FINDING THE JOY WITHIN

A Journey of Identity, Healing, and Self-Discovery

Joy Makepeace

ISBN: 978-0-646-74001-0

Published by Joy Makepeace
Printed in Australia

First eBook edition, June 2025
First print edition, 2026

ISBN (paperback): 978-0-646-74001-0

Dedication

First and foremost, I am dedicating this book to my children, Jordan, Jay, and Violet. May this book help explain to you who I am.

In writing this book, I had to process my own life memories so I could work out who I am and what I've come here to do. The writing of this book has brought me much-needed personal healing, so secondly, I dedicate this book to myself.

Finally, I dedicate this book to you, the reader, and others who may have walked a similar path. I am using the gift I was born with to offer you a guide to help you find your own purpose and answers to life's questions. I hope my struggles help you work out what path and choices you may want to take, and provide hope for a peace-filled future.

This book has provided me with an opportunity to openly tell my story and have those experiences recorded for my family, friends, and others. My shared thoughts will also help those reading this book learn about my life as a Stolen Generations Aboriginal woman. I hope that all who read this book can take at least one thing away from it and pass that knowledge on to others. In doing so, my dream of writing a book will have been achieved, and my life's purpose to love, heal, and educate others will be fulfilled. Ultimately helping you to find the joy within.

Preface

The book that you are about to read came about after one of life's valleys that I found myself in following the birth of my first son, Jordan. It is only part of my life story, and the rest of the book focuses on the lessons I have learnt along the way. It takes a close look at where I have been, what I have learnt, and where I want to go.

There have been many people who have encouraged me to keep writing this book. Some may be aware of their positive influence, but most will be blissfully unaware of how they have touched my life. Regardless of their contribution, they have helped mould me into the person that I have become. I am forever grateful for their influence, which has helped bring my story to life.

So, thank you to everyone who's been there with and for me, and thank you to my children and my family, who've made the writing of this story possible. Thank you to all my friends who've also been a major part of my life, some of whom have been mentioned in this book; however, there are still many whose stories are for another time.

I am so glad that you have found this book at this exact moment in time, just as it was meant to be.

Table of Contents

PART ONE: Who am I?

Chapter 1
Longing to Belong

"Aboriginal women murdered in Lightning Ridge - Joan Margaret West, aged 39, born 27/4/1942 of New Year's Rush Field was found murdered near her camp during the early hours of the 4th of August 1981 by Sgt. Paul and Snr. Constable Ray Strong. A man aged 22 has been charged with wilful murder and will appear at Walgett Court 5th August 1981."

I could not stop the silent tears streaming down my face. My soul felt empty, my overwhelming feelings could no longer be held back, my body was rocked with heartfelt sobs, years of built-up grief turned into tears that streamed down my black face. Each tear released years of anger, guilt, hatred, sadness, and pain. "Why me, why me, why fucking me?" my mind screamed, and my heart ached. I hated my life, I hated who I was, and I hated this world. Why couldn't I die, why was I left behind to live in this shithole? What was life all about anyway? What was the purpose of me even being here? Nobody cares about me. Nobody truly loves me. I'm just a dumb black woman that doesn't know her place in this messed-up world. Who am I anyway? Surely, after thirty years of living this thing called life, I should know the answers to these questions. But clearly, I didn't. While reading those sickening and heart wrenching words in the newspaper article about my mum's death, I knew in that moment that this was just the beginning of a journey I desperately needed to undertake if I was going to find out who I really was.

My mum was born Joan Margaret West on 27 April 1942. As far as the family knows, this is correct, although we have seen other dates and years listed in records. She was the daughter of Bindi West, my grandfather from Bollon, south-western Queensland (QLD) and Terrisa Captain, my grandmother from Mitchell, south-western Queensland. They were both proud Aboriginal people who spent much of their adult lives raising their family in the Aboriginal missions at Brewarrina and Goodooga. My mum, Joan, was born in Goodooga, New South Wales, which is in Kamilaroi Country, also known as Gamilaraay, Gomeroi and by other variations. I don't know much more about her history, only what I have read or been told. By the time I was thirty years old, I had only seen one picture of my mum, and it is a picture that I cherish. Yet no matter how hard, or how long, I stared at that picture, it never told me the answers I was searching for.

I don't know much about my father, other than that he was white. His name was William Bruce Latham and, for some reason, I never felt the urge to look for him. I don't even know if he is still alive. He was not recorded on my original birth certificate and the New South Wales Department of Children's Services, commonly known as DOCS, was unable to release any further information about him.

I am the ninth-born of twelve Aboriginal children and unfortunately none of us grew up with our mum. We became wards of the state, fostered, or adopted, although two of the boys grew up with their birth father and that side of the family. We are what are now commonly known in Australia as members of the Stolen Generations. We did not all have the same birth fathers. I am the second-youngest of the twelve children; this is because my younger siblings are triplets. Out of respect for all my siblings, I write about them with care. Since we were separated from our mum's care at different times and under different circumstances, I can speak only from my own perspective and from knowledge drawn from my DOCS records and personal memories.

My eleven siblings, from eldest to youngest, are: Wayne (deceased), Beverley, David, Valerie, Michael (Mick), Robert (Bob), Rosalind (deceased), William (Billy) (deceased), (Me), Olive, George (Jordie) and Norman (Ben). Even though these are all my birth brothers and sisters, and I know all their names, I still have not had the opportunity to meet them all. Two of them, unfortunately, passed away before I met them, and I only met our brother David for the first time in September 2024. He was sixty-three years old.

Records from DOCS showed that, within a week of being discharged from Wee Waa Hospital in New South Wales, my mum returned me, stating that she would come back for me. According to the records, by the next day I had appeared before the court, accompanied by an officer of the department, and was charged as a neglected child under incompetent guardianship. Within six weeks of this ruling, I was committed to the care of the Minister as a ward of the state and was taken to Myee, which is a departmental home. After a month, I was placed in the care of my first foster family, but, according to records, that foster mother expressed concern about my birth mum's proximity to the foster home and asked that I be returned to the department. I often wonder what happened to me, baby Joy, during those unknown months. Was I scared and lonely? It's weird because I have no conscious memory of that time, but my gut tells me it was scary for me. I'm petrified of a pitch-black room and, still to this day, I always have a night-light on to keep away the fear of the dark.

On 2 August 1972, when I was five months old, I was placed with my future adoptive parents, the Makepeace family. They were recent English immigrants. They had been living in Australia for only five years. Records show that, as I grew older, the Makepeace family made enquiries about adopting me, as they were anxious to make me an official part of their family. Despite their wishes, my birth mum would not consent to my adoption. Knowing this brings me a sense of peace, as it speaks volumes and lets me know that Mum really did not want to willingly give us kids away. That choice was taken from her.

In October 1977, when I was five years old, my birth mum visited the local departmental welfare offices in Moree (New South Wales) and requested photographs of all her children, especially the younger ones. My mum would regularly enquire about our welfare and the possibility of having her children returned to her care. When I look back now, I now know that this was never going to happen. The excuse they gave mum was that, due to her poor mental health and lack of suitable accommodation, our return to her care was highly unlikely. The records say that Mum had schizophrenia and needed hospitalisation for this condition from time to time. Apart from the first week of my life, I never got to meet my mum again before she was brutally murdered by her de facto partner who was 20 years younger than her. He was not the father of any of us children. Within a year of her death, in 1982, the Makepeace family adopted me. I was ten years old at the time.

Looking back, I now know that my life, from the outside, appeared normal. But normal for who? A white middle-class family? It was not until I got into my teenage years that I began to question my identity and started to wonder who I really was, where I was from, and what was life all about anyway. These were the questions that haunted me for years. Finding the answer to "Who am I?" has driven my personal journey of healing and my need to share my experience.

Chapter 2
Bliss in the Unknown

Despite having what I thought was a good upbringing, and knowing I had always been genuinely loved and wanted by a loving family, I knew, deep within my soul, that there was an inner emotional battle going on. On the outside, my life was all roses, yet on the inside, my heart and soul were being ripped apart by a hungry beast demanding to be fed answers.

My adoptive family consisted of my mum, dad, one older sister, two older brothers, and an uncle. My sister Kate is the eldest, followed by my brothers Fenwick and Robert. I was the baby of the family. Both Kate and Fenwick are quite a bit older than me, by twelve to fourteen years, and I don't really remember them being around much while I was growing up. Kate went to boarding school when I was young. She later became a nurse and then moved away from home to work. Fenwick also moved out of home when he was eighteen years old to work in a sawmill. That just left Robert and me at home. Robert is six years older than me, and I remember following him around like a shadow, much to his dislike.

I was five years old the first time I realised my skin was a different colour to the rest of my adoptive family. Mum was washing my hair in the bath, and I asked, "Why is my skin a different colour to your skin, Mum?" I can't remember Mum's exact answer, but it was something evasive, like, "Oh Joy stop worrying, you're always worrying, just wash your hair and get out before the bath water gets cold." Mum was always good at distracting me during awkward moments. My adoptive family didn't see colour. So, despite looking quite different, I was openly accepted as being no different and as part of the family. I am sure that, while I was young, it was comforting to feel so accepted, but as I grew older, I was no longer colour-blind and I knew that, despite being similar in certain ways, I was very different in others, especially in the colour of my skin. No matter how hard my adoptive family tried to convince me that I was the same as them, I knew that something was not the same, and I felt like something was missing. I can't even remember being told that I was adopted, and I don't remember being told that I was Aboriginal either. I just knew I looked and felt different. It wasn't until I was a teenager that I even realised what being Aboriginal meant.

As the baby of the Makepeace family, I was very spoilt. I don't mean that I was spoilt with fine or expensive things; I mean that I always knew I was loved, and that was good enough for me. Surprisingly, I don't think that any of my siblings were ever jealous of me for being so spoilt. Everyone simply accepted me as being special.

My adoptive mum, Audrey, was a stay-at-home mum and was always there for the whole family whenever we needed her. Mum was a beautiful person who would do anything for anyone and could certainly get things done when she put her mind to it. Mum was undoubtedly the backbone of the family. She made all those special occasions memorable. Christmas, Easter, birthdays, and holidays were always so exciting, and I could hardly wait for them to come around.

I always remember the excitement I felt leading up to one of those times, simply because I knew that it wouldn't just be another day. Mum would make sure it was the best day ever, and we would all have fun. Even though we didn't have a great deal of money, Mum somehow always made something from nothing. She hand-knitted jumpers, baked cakes, hand-sewed clothes, painted my bedroom, played cards and board games with me for hours, and taught me so many things about making the most of what you've got. What she really taught me was gratitude. Be grateful for the small things in life, because they really are the big things.

I remember one time Mum took my brother Robert and me to the "drive-in" theatre. Australian, or commonly known as Aussie, drive-ins are big out-door cinemas where you drive your car into a big car parking area and park in front of a huge screen. Back in the day, you put a speaker in the car window so you could hear the movie and watch it from the comfort of your car. I was so excited because we hardly ever got to go to the drive-in. On this night, Mum drove us an hour from our country property near Proston in Queensland, which was sixty-five kilometres from the larger town of Kingaroy, just so we could watch the new release of "Jungle Book". The only problem was that, when we got there, it started to rain. Well, it wasn't so much the rain that was the problem, but the fact that the windscreen wipers on the car didn't work. As we sat there, all three of us squashed into the front bench seat of our old Holden station wagon, Mum decided that since we'd come to watch the movie, we weren't going to miss it. Suddenly, Mum jumped out of the car into the pouring rain, took off her underslip from beneath her skirt, and promptly started wiping down the windscreen with it. Mum continued to jump out into the rain to wipe the windscreen every five minutes until the movie finished! The journey home that night was also interesting because Mum already wore glasses and her night vision was poor. Somehow, we made it home in peace, not pieces. This gives just a small sign of the level of dedication my mum would go to, just to make us kids happy.

On 10 February 2012, my mum sadly lost her battle with bowel cancer. I was nearly 40 years old. Despite being grateful to have had my mum with me for forty years of my life, I couldn't imagine a day without her constantly being there, and I selfishly wished she'd been able to stay with me for longer. It was the saddest day of my life. I felt like an abandoned, frightened little girl, lost in a dark forest in the middle of winter, not knowing what the future would hold without the one person who knew me inside out and loved me unconditionally. I miss her so much and wish that she were still here, so I could just spend another minute with her again. There's nothing I wouldn't give to have another cup of hot Milo while sitting in her lounge room, telling her everything that was happening in my life. She was a special lady who made me into the person that I am today. Mum taught me how to be a good mum. She taught me how to work hard and how to be generous with others without expectations. I love you, Mum, and I thank you for giving me all those wonderful, priceless experiences, memories, and values, which I will forever cherish as they sit safely in my heart, memory, and soul.

My adoptive Dad's name was Fen, short for Fenwick. He was a carpenter by trade and a hard worker who loved a nice beer, usually a home brew, after a full day's work. He was great with all of us kids; he was a real family man. Dad had a strange, witty sense of humour and loved to have a sing-along and a laugh. Usually when he was happily drunk. I always remember that he would sing a song called "Big Rock Candy Mountain" which always put a smile on my face because it made no sense and had funny lyrics. It was only recently that I realised this wasn't a song my dad had made up in his eccentric mind, but in fact a real song. Whenever he had time, we were always off together on an exciting adventure. I can remember Dad spending quality time with me, doing things for me or making things for me. He would take me fishing, make me a kite, teach me how to ride my bike, plant a veggie patch, and build my cubby houses, sometimes even in a tree.

One time Dad and I did a ten-kilometre walk-a-thon together. I was only ten years old and got very tired very quickly, so Dad let me climb onto his back and gave me a piggyback until I had enough energy to walk a little more. He'd get me to chase his shadow on the road, to distract me from the fact that I was exhausted. We did eventually cross the finish line together, holding hands, proud as punch. Without me even knowing it, Dad taught me that if you're going to start a race, it's important that you finish it, no matter what. It doesn't matter if you win or lose; persistence and commitment are the key. This principle has helped me achieve things I could never have dreamed of as a child. Dad was also an avid reader, and I suspect my love of books and learning comes from his enthusiasm for knowledge. Dad used to give me the biggest bear hugs that nearly squeezed the life out of me. I used to look at my dad and think he was so smart, but as an adult, I felt like he had died with his talents still inside him. In Dad's earlier years, he had been in the Navy, and later in life he'd worked as a psychiatric nurse, an artist, wood carver, and a carpenter. Dad knew how to build houses, chisel intricate wood carvings, paint landscapes, and build model boats. Once he even built a sandstone fireplace. He'd spend hours reading textbooks about the universe and towards the end of his life he became fascinated with quantum physics. Yet here he was, hidden away from the world in small country towns around New South Wales and Queensland, with that philosophical knowledge going to waste. In retrospect, I can see how soul-destroying being stuck in a rut can be. This explains why he was so proud of all my achievements, especially my academic studies. I remember mum telling me that when they got me as a five-month-old baby, the DOCS paperwork said I was retarded (I hate that word). Apparently, Dad would not accept that diagnosis and made it his personal goal to give me the best start in life and prove the DOCS social workers wrong. I'm pretty sure he did. What I now know is that I probably had what is known as global development delays, and with lots of care, love, and positive attention, my adoptive family helped to close that gap, and I managed to catch up with the other kids who were my age.

My mum and dad split up when I was fourteen years old. I was so torn whether to move to Adelaide with my mum or stay in Queensland with my dad. I chose to move to Adelaide, and from that moment my relationship with Dad gradually grew more distant. I felt crushed when I heard that my dad had passed away in 2018. This was six years after mum had passed away. I was forty-six years old, and I didn't consciously think about it too much at the time, but in the back of my mind I realised that I was now an orphan. I no longer had any parents alive — birth or adoptive. A deep sense of abandonment swept over me the day my dad died. I will always love you, Dad with all my heart, and I thank you for giving me a passion for learning and a creative mind. I really felt loved by you and wish I'd loved you more in return. Rest in peace Dad, you did well.

Another member of our family was my Uncle Cecil, who initially was a friend of the Makepeace family. He immigrated with the family from England and just never left, until twenty years later when he ran away with my mum and later became my stepdad. Yes, at the time it was a scandal, but to me, I had always known him, so I didn't have an issue having him as my stepdad. Strangely enough the change of his relationship with mum wasn't too weird for me to accept.

Uncle was a mechanic by trade; he too was a very hard worker. He was a very tall man, with big strong hands. He and

I would go on long hikes through the mid-north coast of New South Wales countryside, and my little hand would hold on tight to his as we walked along together enjoying the scenery. I remember he used to say, "If you want a job done well, then do it yourself." I never understood what that really meant as a child. But I certainly live by that rule now. I'm not a perfectionist, but I am a bit obsessive about things being done a certain way. Okay, okay, so I am a perfectionist! I'm going to blame my uncle for sharing this trait. I remember sitting on Uncle's lap every evening to watch my favourite TV shows like "Basil Brush;" "Some Mothers Do 'Ave 'Em", "The Two Ronnies", or "Hey Hey It's Saturday". I don't know how Uncle could put up with my endless questions … "so what's happening now? What does that mean? What are they doing now?" Now that I am a parent, I can imagine how annoying that must have been, but he was patient - up to a point. Then I knew it was time to just be quiet, watch and listen. My uncle passed away in a nursing home in Adelaide, South Australia in 2002, with Mum right by his side. Mum and he spent fifteen loving years together, which seemed like they'd waited and wasted so many years before they could openly show and share their true love. It didn't make any sense to me. Mum survived another ten lonely years without him. I love and miss you, Uncle. Thank you for teaching me to be strong, independent, well organised, and, unfortunately, very impatient. Finally, together forever with Mum.

My sister Kate is fourteen years older than me, so there is quite an age gap. Despite this, I looked up to her. I used to think that Kate always led such an exciting life, like one of those characters you watch on a television soap opera. I can remember that she always had a car, a boyfriend, and her best friend at her disposal. She would come and go like the wind, and we always had so much fun while she was home. Kate has a strange sense of humour like Dad, and it quite often felt like she was cooking up mischief, just like a witch. You know, hubble, bubble, boil, and trouble? Her wicked, yet infectious laugh would echo through the house, with her long fingernails, and thick hair she could most definitely pass as a witch. Kate showed me how to be carefree, adventurous, and a strong, independent, fun-loving, free-spirited, resourceful, beautiful woman. She always had her best friend Janice by her side, and I consider Janice to be my other big sister too. Thank you for teaching me how to take care of myself, how to follow my dreams, and how to be a lady when need be. I love you Kate, you're my idol and one-of-a-kind. I wouldn't trade you for anything.

My brother Fenwick had the same name as Dad. Fenwick is twelve years older than me, so he didn't spend too much time at home with me either. I do remember that he was a devoted St George Dragons Rugby League supporter. One time, he asked Mum if he could paint his room red and white, the same colours as the Mighty Dragons. Mum agreed; however, it wasn't just a little bit of red and mostly white — it was the other way around: bright red walls and a little bit of white, too in-ya-face for my liking.

There was no way I would have let Fenwick know I wasn't a Dragons fan, otherwise I'd have been dealt a relentless tickling session that wouldn't have ceased until I had yielded to the Mighty Dragons. When Fenwick was in his early twenties, he had a terrible sawmill accident and accidentally cut off three of his fingers on his left hand. I remember that he had to sell his big Holden Statesmen car because it didn't have any power steering, and he had to get a small Datsun Stanza to accommodate his new life with a disability. He later got a job in an office with Veterans' Affairs, but that was certainly not my brother's style. Before the accident, he was left-handed, like me, and he was a very talented artist like dad. Prior to the accident, he could sketch portraits by hand like a photograph. Through rehabilitation, he learnt to use his right hand but never regained the full artistic drawing potential like he previously had. Later in life he moved to Tasmania and became a well-known potter. His talent and resilience in the face of adversity never cease to amaze me. Never once did he give up hope, hold resentment, or let life get the better of him. Now he has established himself as a driving instructor, mainly for recently arriving immigrants from culturally diverse backgrounds. Fenwick has taught me to never ever give up. To always try your hardest and use the gifts that God — or, according to Fenwick's beliefs, Hare Krishna — has given you to the best of your ability. He's also taught me to do what makes you happy — maybe not rich, but happy. Fenwick, you are an amazingly talented artist and a dedicated partner, dad, and grandfather who can imagine beyond the everyday world and through your art you speak to people's hearts. Your art not only saved your own life, but many others too. I know we don't live in each other's pockets, but I promise you that you live in my heart and I love you lots.

My brother Robert is six years older than me, and I spent more time growing up with Robert than with either Kate or Fenwick. In my earlier years, I was Robert's little shadow. We went to the same schools, and he would always defend me when the white kids would call me a racist name like a boong or coon. Those derogatory racist names were common back then. Thankfully, there are now laws in place to address the offensive use of those outdated hate speech words. Robert took the law into his own hands when we were kids. It was called a knuckle sandwich — or a fair punch in the nose. Robert was one of those cool guys who would have all the girls hanging off him. Although most boys would envy him, he was never really interested in dating girls because he was sports-crazy and preferred playing and watching cricket or rugby rather than going out with girls.

Robert has a weird sense of humour. It seems to run in the Makepeace family. I remember on one occasion when he broke his foot while playing rugby and had to go to hospital and stay for a couple of days. He was sixteen years old, and they put his leg in plaster and supported it in traction. While recovering, the nurses had to keep checking that his toes were warm and to make sure that he still had feeling in them. Well, what did Robert do? He asked mum to buy him one of those squishy plastic little monsters that used to fit on the end of those big old thick pencils. Naively, mum did as he asked, only to be told the next day that one of the nurses nearly had a heart attack when she put her hand under the sheets to do his regular toe check and felt this gruesome thing on the end of his toe. Robert got a laugh out of that one. They do say laughter is good medicine; I reckon he was just trying to get better sooner.

I must admit that Robert does tend to be accident-prone. I can honestly say that Robert has had more injuries than I've had hot dinners. He's had stitches from when Fenwick threw a table tennis bat at his head, broken countless bones, and had too many car crashes to remember. He did roll his Mini Moke, which doesn't even have a roof, a couple of times, and yet he still managed to walk away unscathed. He nearly cut his hand off at work when he was about thirty years old, and still today he seems to try to unintentionally assassinate himself, whether by electrocution, death by chainsaw, or simply slipping on a banana skin. Despite being the typical example of Mr Accident Prone, he is also like a cat with nine lives and bounces back after every incident. Robert has taught me to never take life too seriously, and that if you get wounded, just patch it up. She'll be right mate. He's also proven that everyone needs a good mate in life. I love you Robert and I know you have always been there for me, and I know you always will be, so thank you my big brother. I forgive you for the times you've accidentally or purposefully hurt me.

What has become clear to me through writing about my adoptive brothers and sister is how much I don't know about my birth family. There are so many people out there who have their birth families at their fingertips and yet they still take them for granted. They end up falling out and arguing over petty, unimportant things and they act like they hate each other. They spend their entire lives ignoring each other because of their stubborn pride. This is sad, and it just reminds me that life is too short to be wasting precious time on such petty things. Yet we all seem to do it.

I am eternally grateful for all the memories I have shared with my adoptive family, but I know that there will always be questions about how my life would have been different had I not been adopted and if I had grown up with my birth family. I have accepted that being adopted was my destiny. I am also sure that being Aboriginal, which is a vastly different culture to that of my English born adoptive family, has strongly driven my desire to strengthen my Aboriginal cultural connections and discover a true sense of belonging. The one thing I know for sure is that being adopted has strengthened my appreciation of family. My adoptive name — Joy Makepeace — is very apt for me, as I see myself as the one person that keeps the peace and often tries to mend the rifts and bring the family back together. Yet I'm not an angel and there are exceptions to that rule.

When I was nine years old, we were living in New South Wales, in a small town called Nundle, about an hour from Tamworth. My mum and dad were the caretakers of the local caravan park, and we lived in a huge on-site caravan. I distinctly remember the regular visits that we would get from my caseworker at the New South Wales welfare department – formally known as the Department of Children's Services (DOCS).

The caseworker's name was Brian, and he would come to our caravan while I ate baked beans on toast for lunch. He would ask me questions like, "Are you happy living with the Makepeace family? Do you like school? Do you have lots of friends? Is this where you sleep?" Brian never fazed me with his questions, nor did I wonder why he was there or why he was asking those sorts of questions. I do remember telling him that I wanted to be a hairdresser when I grew up.

It's only as an adult that I have discovered, and was quite amazed by, the large amount of information and records NSW Welfare has kept on me. The stack of records is remarkably high. The reason for all these visits was that I was still a ward of the state and therefore still legally had to be regularly checked on as part of the department's responsibility and duty of care towards me. I always gave glowing reports for Brian to take back to his office to add to my ever-growing file. It still amazes me to this day that the reason for removal was often listed as "in the best interest of the child". I often wonder whether this statement was ever found to be true.

I remember the day that Brian came to tell me that my birth mum had died. I was nine years old. The information didn't really sink in at all, and I felt no real grief at the time of hearing this news. As I had never even met my mum, only as a baby and had since been protected from any information about who I really was and who my birth family was, I had not been able to strongly develop any attachments with my own birth mum or family. Sadly, even to this day, contact visits between children in care and their birth families are still limited for a variety of reasons, either lack of resources from the department to facilitate regular contact, lack of commitment from the parents, emotional distress and confusion for the children and the department's fear of endangering the children's attachment to the new foster family. This has been researched over the years, but they always base their research on the current children in care. I wonder whether there has even been a longitudinal study capturing a Stolen Generations adult adoptee's memories, thoughts, opinions, and experiences about how regular ongoing access visits, or no access visits impacted their long-term social and emotional wellbeing and identity. I can honestly say that not being given this opportunity through my childhood, to have regular access to my birth family, especially my Aboriginal birth mother, left a deep emotional scar and certainly caused ongoing identity issues and confusion, still to this day. Let's hope that more robust, evidence-based research helps to rectify this cruel, archaic practice in the future. Quite honestly, the child protection system, practices, and policies could do with an entire overhaul.

As a ward of the state, I was asked by my DOCS caseworker if I wanted to go to my mum's funeral. I remember feeling angry and saying to myself, "Why would I want to go to her funeral? I didn't even know or meet her. She didn't care about me." It was a huge decision to make at nine years of age, and one I came to on my own. I didn't go to my birth mum's funeral, and it was a decision I regretted for years. Without even realising it, I had been emotionally beating myself up and carrying guilt for thirty years because I did not attend my mum's funeral. Do you know how emotionally taxing that is? As an adult, I now know how sad, unfortunate, and even disrespectful it was that I did not attend my own mother's funeral. I knew I had to look inside myself and undertake a self-forgiveness exercise to heal the unresolved grief, loss, and self-hate I was experiencing because of this decision, which continued to haunt me. I did eventually forgive myself, but it was only recently that my eyes were truly opened, and my heart was healed about this traumatic childhood memory and belief that I was disrespectful. It took attending my Aboriginal female friend's funeral as an adult for me to finally realise when I was sitting there in the church and secretly getting wild (angry) that the kids that had attended were running around oblivious to the seriousness of the occasion. In that moment, a light bulb went off in my head, and I instantly realised "Oh my goodness, Joy, even if you had decided to go to your mum's funeral, you wouldn't have even realised the significance of it or the respect associated with it. You would have just been like these kids, running around without a worry in the world." I know this doesn't sound like it could have had the impact it had on me, but let me assure you, it did. Sometimes it's that simple when we are open to hearing the messages sent from the Universe, the Source, divine beings, the creators of life, or, alternatively, what is known as Our Dreaming or our Ancestors, and known to many simply as God. At once, I was able to stand back and reflect on all the circumstances surrounding my own mum's funeral from a child's perspective, instead of the view of a wounded adult. This new perspective took thirty years to surface from the depths of my subconscious memories, yet it has given me such peace I am now in a place where, when I read or think about my mum's death, I no longer yearn for a different past. I just accept what happened and there was nothing right or wrong about it, it simply was what it was, and I cannot change it, I can only accept it as it is, and forgive myself for not attending her funeral and not showing her the respect she deserved as the woman who gave me life. I do respect my mum, Joan. I do love her. I do wish that I had met her, and I wish I had been told more stories about her. Despite the small amount of information I do have about my mum, I have still created my own image of her in my mind's eye and those memories are vivid and will forever live in my heart and soul. Until we meet again. Rest in peace, Mum.

Chapter 3
Long Journey Home

I don't think I understood the magnitude of what I should have felt when I first met my younger siblings — the triplets — in 1981. I didn't understand what all the fuss was about and couldn't understand why my adoptive mum was in a meeting at the DOCS office in Moree with all these important yet distressed-looking people. As it turned out, due to the death of our birth mum Joan, the welfare department contacted my adoptive mum and the triplets' two sets of adoptive parents to have a meeting to discuss future contact between our three families. While our adoptive parents were all busy in the meeting room, the triplets and I played happily outside on the lawn together. We were all blissfully unaware of the exact, sad, detailed discussions that were going on. However, it became apparent that because of this meeting, it was decided by the DOCS workers that all three families would try to maintain regular contact with each other in an attempt to keep the "West/Latham" children together and allow us to continue to get to know each other. I think this was encouraged particularly because the triplets and I had the same birth father.

The triplets lived with two families who already knew each other, so they did manage to maintain that regular contact. Unfortunately, this was not to be the case with me, because my family regularly moved around Australia and often the distances between our family and the triplets were vast. Before I knew it, the years just seemed to slip away, and the contact never occurred again until I instigated it when I was in my early twenties.

The next time I really started to wonder about my family and feel the need to find them was during the final six months of my Graduate Diploma in Education at the University of South Australia. I really don't know what triggered this desire; I just know that it was the right time to follow up on what my spirit, the deepest part of who I am, was telling me to do. I only knew it to be my gut instinct back then. It was on 6 July 1993 that I first contacted NSW Link-Up. I'm not even sure how I discovered that there was such an organisation, and I remember not knowing what to expect or even what I was going to achieve by doing this. All I knew was the NSW Link-Up helped Stolen Generations people find and reunite with their birth families.

The only information that I had when I rang NSW Link-Up was an old piece of paper that I'd sneakily found among my adoptive mum's important papers that she stored in an old Cadbury chocolates tin box. This amazing piece of paper listed all my natural siblings' names, birth dates, and places of birth. Unbeknown to me at the time, this invaluable piece of paper was one of the key pieces of information that would help me find my siblings.

When I contacted NSW Link-Up, I desperately wanted to meet up with all my siblings; however, NSW Link-Up managed to contact only my older sister Rosalind who had also registered with them in search of the rest of us. I was also excited to re-establish contact with the triplets, but I discovered that they were concentrating on completing their high school certificate. Out of respect, I did not hassle them during this crucial time in their lives. Locating family and then building a relationship with your birth family doesn't just happen overnight. It takes time, energy, and, particularly patience, which, as mentioned, isn't one of my strong points.

After my first enquiry with NSW Link-Up, it took fourteen months before Rosalind, and I had a reunion. By this stage, I was twenty-two years old. This reunion took place in Wollongong, New South Wales. My then fiancé (whom I will refer to as "Rusty") and I travelled by car from South Australia to meet Rosalind, and I can still remember it as if it were yesterday. We met on the water's edge in a local park in Wollongong. Rosalind had already arrived with her caseworker before I got there. We turned up with another Link-Up caseworker, and we walked over to meet Rosalind.

It was a strange feeling, after all the lead-up to this reunion and I must admit that not all my expectations were met. The one thing that I was wanting was a sense of belonging. For me, personally, I was hoping that Rosalind would at least look a bit like me. For me, that would have been confirmation that we were sisters. However, to my disappointment, I didn't look like Rosalind and, in fact, I don't look like any of my four sisters. I have dark wavy hair, and all my sisters have light brown curly hair. We are all different shapes, sizes, and shades.

Rosalind and I tried hard to have a conversation, but it was difficult to catch up on a lifetime of information within one short afternoon. Rosalind, like all but two of our siblings, had also been fostered and grew up with a non-Aboriginal family. In a way I was disappointed because I had envisaged that when I met Rosalind all my questions were going to get answered. This was not the case because Rosalind also had the same questions about our birth mum and family, to which neither of us knew the answers.

In the past when Stolen Generations topic came up in conversation, you would hear how the birth families all talk about how the child that has been removed holds a special place in the birth family's hearts and memories. You dream that the birth family has just been waiting with open arms for you to return. I'm sure that this is the ultimate dream for every adoptee. However, families who have been torn so far apart physically, psychologically, and geographically, repairing the damage is nearly impossible. Often there is nothing to return to. In our circumstances, who was left to pass on any of the oral history so that we can, in turn, pass it on to our children? Once again there were no simple answers. I could tell it was going to be harder to find out who I was, and where I belonged, than I initially thought it would be.

For Rosalind and me, there seemed to be so many gaps in what we knew about our family. It was a matter of simply relaying information about our lives and sharing any information our foster parents may have shared in relation to our birth family. We tried desperately to match up any information we had relating to our family, but neither of us knew anything for certain.

That morning, we spent time talking together, trying to learn about each other's lives and comparing our upbringings. We looked for similarities but only found differences. It was like being with a total stranger and feeling completely uncomfortable, and filled with guilt, knowing that I should have been feeling a deep, loving connection. After lunch, we went back to Rosalind's little apartment and Rosalind and I talked some more. Rosalind told me that when she was younger, she had given birth to a baby girl. She said that, because she had been a teenager and felt so young, she had given the baby up for adoption. At the time, I must admit, I was shocked, and not having children myself I couldn't imagine ever doing that. I didn't let Rosalind see that I found this deeply confusing considering our own adoption experiences. I tucked this secret thought away in the back of my mind, knowing that one day that little girl would come looking for us. Before we knew it, our reunion had ended. From the perspective of an outsider, this reunion may have seemed just like the beginning, yet it sadly was more like the end of our relationship. On returning to Adelaide, South Australia, Rosalind and I continued to write to each other occasionally. We'd ring each other whenever we could, but gradually over the years our phone calls got less and less. I moved around very often, and the letters got fewer and fewer as it was harder to find me. Sadly, though, we gradually drifted apart. There just wasn't a strong enough bond to keep us in close contact with each other. Despite this lack of ongoing connection, the curiosity I felt about my family and my identity had been temporarily eased and surprisingly I felt a sense of inner peace for a little while longer. I wasn't to know at the time that this would be the first and last time I would meet my sister Rosalind, who sadly passed away from sleep apnoea in 2018. Rest in peace, my darling gentle sister. You deserved better in life, and I wish that I and the world had given it to you.

My next opportunity to meet my birth family came a year later in 1995 while Rusty, whom I had now married, and I were making our way to Queensland to visit my adoptive dad, Fen. This was a special reunion and one that I will always remember. NSW Link-Up was not involved in this reunion; it was simply a chance meeting.

By now, the triplets had finished their studies at high school and Jordie and Ben were working with their adoptive father on their family farm. We decided that we would drop in on the boys' adoptive mother in Dubbo, New South Wales, on our way through to Queensland. She was extremely happy to see us. Thankfully, she took the time to share photos of the triplets from their high school formal and Olive's teenage modelling photographs. These were the first photographs that I had seen of the triplets since I had last seen them when I was nine years old, and they were five. I must admit I felt an immense sense of overwhelming pride seeing my younger brothers and sister all grown up and they all looked so smart, stunning and beautiful in their formal wear. The other amazing thing was that the boys most definitely resembled me. For the first time since childhood, I felt like a piece of my personal jigsaw puzzle had been put back together. The boys' mum gave me the address where the boys and their dad were living and working. Coincidentally, it happened to be in the same New South Wales town that I was born — Wee Waa. My heart filled with joy, and I felt like I was going home to meet them.

Without hesitation, we drove from Dubbo to Wee Waa in the hope of catching up with the boys. When we got to Wee Waa, it was late in the afternoon, and we managed to book into a small local motel. After settling in, we went down the street to the local phone box (no mobile phones back then) and tried to call the boys before we dropped in, as their property was out of town. I was disappointed when no one answered the phone, so we decided to sit in the car for a while before giving the boys another call.

While we were sitting there waiting, someone who looked just like my brother Jordie, and another young man, walked straight past our car. I excitedly screamed, "Look, look, I think that's Jordie!" Rusty thought that I was going crazy, but for the sake of peace, he humoured me, and we jumped out of the car like a couple of private-eye detectives and followed the poor unsuspecting boys into the local café.

I hurriedly sat down on an angle where I could see them, but they couldn't really see me. Still unsure of whether I was being ridiculous and just imagining that this could be Jordie, I sat there like a giggling little schoolchild with my nerves fully charged. Rusty, still believing that I was surely losing it, decided that if we were going to sit there in a café, then he may as well fill his belly. I was too nervous to eat, so I just continued to evaluate the situation from a safe distance. I could hear my inner voice asking, "Should I? Shouldn't I?" Then I told the voice in my head, "If you don't do it Joy, you're gonna regret it". "But what if he rejects me? Or even worse, tells me to piss off. Or what if he pretends, he doesn't know who I am? Go on, ya know ya gotta do it. What's the worst thing that could happen? Just bloody hurry up and do it before they walk out the door and ya miss ya chance. Stop being so bloody stupid, Joy, just do it. Ya know ya want to!" I knew I had to do it; I hadn't come this far to simply walk away. I knew I was about to make a complete fool of myself and approach a stranger and ask him if he is one of my baby brothers whom I hadn't seen since I was nine years old.

Finally, the curiosity just got the better of me because I could see that their meal was quickly ending. I knew in my heart that I couldn't live with myself if I missed this last chance. I took a big breath and, with a big push from Rusty, got to my feet. With my legs feeling like jelly and my belly feeling like it was full of eels, I marched right over to their table and blurted out, "Excuse me, is your name Jordie?" It felt like an eternity, yet it was only a split second before he simply replied in a country drawl, "So you must be the big sister then!" Oh, what a relief, and yet a let-down, all in one. I was relieved that I'd got the right person, yet once again it wasn't really the arms-open, welcoming, homecoming reunion I'd envisaged. Don't get me wrong, he was pleased to see me, but it was more of a shock than anything for both of us. He clearly wasn't a hugger like me. Anyway, after a quick catch-up we arranged a time to properly meet him out at the farm later that night. With that arranged, we once again went our separate ways.

By the time we found our way out to their farm, it was pitch-black, and we thought we were surely going to get lost. In our attempt to check our bearings, we pulled into another farm owner's yard to see whether we were heading in the right direction. When we told the owners who we were looking for, they invited us in and gave us further directions. While standing in this complete stranger's kitchen, the weirdest thing happened. The woman just stared at me, tilted her head, and then said, "Have I met you before?" I knew that it wasn't one of those occasions where I could have met or seen this person before around the local shops, because I had travelled from Adelaide and had never been back to this small town since I was born. I knew in an instant that the reason this lady thought that she had met me before was because I reminded her of the boys. My mind was racing with thoughts: "Oh my goodness, she thinks I look like the boys. She can tell just by looking at me that I'm their sister. Oh my goodness, I can't believe that I look like someone. Oh my goodness, this is the best feeling I've ever had in my whole life. Thank you, thank you, thank you!

Without any knowledge of my internal chatter, this woman was unaware that she'd just granted me one of the most amazing gifts in my life — an overwhelming sense of belonging. The fact that a stranger had recognised our likeness was just so emotionally comforting, rewarding and reassuring for me. I nearly cried, yet I puffed up my chest with an unbelievable sense of pride and said, "No, I don't think we've ever met before, but I'm Jordie and Ben's big sister, Joy." I could see by the expression on her face that she was really confused. Usually, it's the other way round, as when my adoptive white brother Robert or mum would introduce me to their friends, "This is my baby sister or my daughter, Joy." Without any explanation that I'm adopted, it's interesting to watch the expression on a stranger's face; you can almost see the cogs of their brain ticking over, trying to figure it all out. For me, I didn't care what Jordie and Ben's neighbours thought, all I knew was I finally felt a sense of belonging. It was the homecoming that I needed to refill my spirit!

With clear directions and a new sense of enthusiasm and excitement, I could hardly contain myself as we jumped back in the car and eventually managed to find Jordie that night. Unfortunately, my other brother Ben was not home, and I didn't get the chance to meet him again, despite it being fourteen years since our first meeting. Jordie, his adoptive dad, Rusty and I sat around the kitchen table that night and once again talked small talk and tried to catch up on too many years of separation. It was just replenishing to be simply in the presence of one of my brothers. I just sat there, soaking in every moment of the reunion, never wanting to leave, but knowing it would have to end.

I must admit that as we left Wee Waa, I went away with a renewed sense of satisfaction that must have been quite strong, as it carried me through another four years before I once again felt the urge to resume searching for the rest of my birth family.

Things happen for a reason, and I attract situations into my life that provide me with the opportunities I need to learn and grow from those experiences. I'm sure this is exactly what happened to me when I came across a job that was advertised for the South Australia Link-Up Caseworker position. At the time I was self-employed and worked from home doing beauty therapy and massages, while also looking after our son, Jordan, who was born in 1996 and was now three years old. I had recently completed my certificate in beauty therapy and had done part-time work for a large Adelaide-based natural skincare business, but financially we'd been struggling, so it was time to look for a "real job."

I remember it was on a Saturday morning, and I was reading the local Adelaide newspaper The Advertiser, when I saw the South Australia Link-Up caseworker position advertised. Ever since I had my own reunion with the help of NSW Link-Up; I had been intrigued with becoming a caseworker. At the time, South Australia didn't have a large Link-Up program, and it was managed through the Department of Health — Adoptions and Family Information Services. There was only one position, and it was low-key. It was so tucked away in the newspaper that even the Aboriginal community were hardly aware that it existed. Once again, I felt like the Universe and our Ancestors were keeping that position safe just for me to win.

Despite having few qualifications in this field, other than my own Stolen Generations and adoption experience and a couple of years of project work, I decided to apply and give it my best shot. That is exactly what I did. Fortunately, fate was on my side, and I won a position as a caseworker with the South Australia Link-Up Program in February 1999. In this position, I helped Aboriginal clients who had been removed from their families to find their families and reunite them. This role was most definitely close to my heart, and it was a position I took very seriously. The first year we spent setting up the service.

It was during this time that I felt the need to search for my family again. I had already met Rosalind and the triplets, so this left five older brothers and two older sisters who I was yet to meet. With the support of South Australia Link-Up, I registered as a client in the hope that I could find and be reunited with Wayne, David, Bob, Mick, Beverley, Valerie, and Billy.

I knew that the first major task would be trying to track down my siblings, keeping in mind that we all had our names changed and had either been adopted, fostered, or grown up with different families around Australia. Thankfully, I had already applied to DOCS and had all my documents and records at my fingertips. I knew all my brother and sister's birth names and dates of birth, but not all their current names. This made things difficult.

It was now a matter of sifting through my records and searching through electoral roll records to find a match. This was a very tedious task and took more time than my impatient self wanted. Eventually, the South Australia Link-Up staff did find a lead or two and I finally had contact details for Beverley, David, Mick, Bob, Jordie, Ben, and Olive. Sadly, during this searching process, the Link-Up staff discovered and told me that my eldest brother Wayne had passed away when he was in his twenties. It was gut-wrenching to discover this. I felt like a piece of me had also died. It seemed silly to feel such a sense of loss for someone who I'd never even met and only known as a name on paper, but at the same time I knew my feelings were very real and completely understandable.

Knowing that Wayne died before I got to meet him caused the deep sense of grief and loss that I felt for our mum to resurface. Once the shock had subsided and the tears ceased to flow, it just made my determination to meet the rest of my family that much stronger. I knew that time was of the essence because we just never know what the future has in store for us. Sadly, our brother Billy also passed away unexpectedly in April 2011, before we all got to meet him. I did, however, thankfully and respectfully, get to go to his memorial service to represent our family and pay our respects and say our last hello and goodbyes to our beautiful brother Bill. I'll share more about that special day at the end of this chapter.

Since meeting my sister Rosalind and my brother Jordie, time had quickly flown by. I was now 28 years old, and I was married and had my own son, whom we called Jordan who was now four years old. Rusty and I decided on one of our trips through to Queensland to visit my dad, Fen, that we would try and meet my brother Bob for the first time.

I remember that Bob lived in rural country New South Wales, and we had to travel along a dirt road for what seemed like forever, to get to his little country cottage. When we got there, it was in the afternoon just before dusk. His partner Louella was home, but Bob was still at work driving the tractor in a paddock somewhere nearby. When Louella met me, she had the same look on her face that the neighbour to Jordie and Ben's farm had. It was an, "Oh my goodness you look just like your brother." I remember Louella contacting Bob and saying, "Bob, your sister Joy's here, and she looks just like you." Meeting Bob was everything I dreamed of. He gave me a big welcoming hug and had the biggest smile. We talked for hours, and they invited us to stay a few nights. Jordan was so in awe of his Uncle Bob, and they were like two peas in a pod. He followed his Uncle Bob around like a shadow and I knew their bond would be strong for life. We headed off on our travels knowing that this would be the first of many reunions, as we had a strong connection.

By now I had met with Rosalind, Bob, and Jordie, as adults, and Ben and Olive when we were children, but I was still yet to meet David, Mick, Beverley, Valerie, as mentioned, sadly both Billy and Wayne had passed before I could meet them.

I know most people would say, "just get over it", and don't understand what all the fuss is about, but I can guarantee that it isn't as simple and straightforward as rocking up and saying "Hi, how ya been? Put the kettle on, won't ya?" There is an overwhelming sense of fear that grips you like an iron fist and can stop you from moving forward. I know that it seems crazy to fear your own family, but when you've never met someone before, all the old fears of being rejected or abandoned again raise their ugly heads. "What if they don't like me? What if they think that I'm too white? What if they never want to see me again? What if they think I'm a snob?" All these thoughts constantly swim around in your mind. To help overcome these crippling thoughts, I had lots of counselling leading up to each of my reunions. This certainly helped, but it didn't stop the endless, crazy, fear-of-rejection thoughts jumping around in my head.

New South Wales and South Australia Link-Up oversaw the arrangements for the big reunion, which was to be held in Dubbo, New South Wales in 2002. The caseworkers ensured that we made about four phone calls to each other. Every time I spoke with another sibling, my heart did the exact same thing. It began to race with anticipation, my voice became shaky, my palms were sweaty, and I could hardly hold the phone. I just knew that I didn't make any sense at all. Each time I felt like I reverted to my childhood, and I felt just like a little girl going to "big" school for the first time. Thankfully, there were always questions to ask and to answer, so often the conversation would flow freely, despite all my earlier fears.

Now, during the middle of this critical time in my life, my marriage was dissolving. I was experiencing a complete identity crisis and didn't even know it at the time. Just when I felt like I was regaining my birth family, my own little family was falling apart. So, despite feeling like I was on an isolated island surrounded by sharks, no way was I going to miss the bigger family reunion in Dubbo, New South Wales. At the time, my son Jordan was five years old, and I was twenty-nine. Despite being once again thoroughly scared of rejection, I was too excited to let the fear stop me from going. To be truthful, my thoughts were so absorbed by the reunion that everything else, including my marriage, took second priority. I didn't have time to deal with my confused emotions, so deeply buried the guilt of my decisions in the depths of my mind and soul.

When all of us brothers and sisters arrived in Dubbo, I don't think any of us knew what was in store for us. We just went there hoping that it would all be OK. The big reunion was so well planned that we need not have worried or feared. There were three Link-Up caseworkers present, and a counsellor was also available. We arranged our first meeting at a neutral place along the Macquarie River that runs through Dubbo. There was a park where our kids could play, and a barbeque to cook up a deadly "good" feed, once we'd all arrived and had our first introductions.

The emotions that flowed on that day were like the waves of the ocean. They just kept rolling in and pounding us with one wave of emotion after another; it never seemed to stop. Despite having previously talked on the phone with each of my siblings, there were still overwhelming emotions that opened like floodgates as soon as I saw and cuddled each sibling and held them close to my heart.

I remember sitting on the picnic table with my back to the car park, wanting to look, but feeling the familiar heart-pounding sensation. From that moment on, I can't exactly remember everything that happened. This seemed ridiculous because it had been the moment I'd been looking forward to my whole life. I do remember that when I met my big sister

Beverley, it felt like a homecoming. I threw my arms around her and never wanted to let go. We cried and cried, and it felt like a lifetime of never knowing each other melted away in a moment. Despite growing up separately, we were kindred spirits, and I knew we were sisters and meant to be together. The best part was that our kids were there, and they got to meet their cousins for the first time too. Knowing my siblings and cousins was something that I'd always yearned for as a child and I'm so grateful that I'd managed to do it for my own son, Jordan, and years later for my other children, Jay and Violet.

Throughout the afternoon, the reunions just kept happening one after the other, and before long we had all congregated and shared lots of hugs, love, and tears. We spent from the afternoon right through to dusk just getting to know each other and endlessly talking. There was so much to learn about each other, and no one wanted it to end. The sun was quickly going down, and I remember that I had met Beverley, Valerie, Mick and Bob, and we were all waiting on Olive and Jordie. Unfortunately, David, Rosalind, Billy and Ben didn't make this reunion.

Before our reunion, Olive and I had been writing to each other, and I loved receiving her letters. She would always choose lovely paper that always had a lovely powdered floral scent that reminded me of a favourite aunty. I was unsure whether Olive would be able to join us at the reunion, so it came as a beautiful surprise when she turned up with her adoptive mum and dad. It was lovely to meet Olive once again and I couldn't believe how much she had grown up in those twenty-one years since I'd last seen her in Moree when our mum had passed away. Olive appeared so stable-headed, calm, centred, poised, and elegant. While we three sisters were sitting on the grass, eating our barbeque with our plates of food balanced on our laps, for the first time in my life, I felt complete. I felt an overwhelming sense of pride. It felt so right, and my heart was singing with joy. We were just missing our sister Rosalind, and it would have been picture perfect.

I distinctly remember my brother Jordie turning up to the reunion. You could hardly miss him, or should I say, you could hardly miss hearing the roaring exhaust system on his Holden Ute. It was like something out of a "Mad Max" film. It had spotlights as big a dinner plates, exhausts, aerials galore, stickers all over the back window, mudflaps big enough for a Mack truck; a roo (kangaroo) bar that would scare a buffalo away, and a CB radio just in case of emergency. When he stepped out of his ute, he walked with a swagger like he was about to draw out his pistols and shoot someone. He had a big cowboy hat and a pair of matching boots. He looked as Aussie outback as they come. He certainly made an impression. I know that Mick and Bob were happy to finally meet him, and they spent much of the time catching up and talking about blokey things. I can't really remember having a detailed conversation with Jordie this time, but I was just grateful he made the effort to come. When I named my son Jordan, I didn't realise that I had, in fact, named him after one of my brothers, whom I had known as "George" but was also nicknamed Jordie. It was a strange coincidence.

Our brother David had initially decided to come to the Dubbo reunion, but unfortunately (despite Link-Up having booked his ticket and accommodation) he was unable to make it to meet the rest of us in Dubbo. I was heartbroken. All the other plans had run so smoothly with the reunion. I was so disappointed for myself, but I felt disappointment for David. I felt so powerless to help reassure him that everything would be OK, and we were all in the same boat (feeling scared) and we could do this together. It wasn't to be, and I am happy to say that we had our first reunion with our sixty-three-year-old brother David in Walgett in September 2024. Our brother Ben also didn't make it to the Dubbo reunion. I am not sure why and was so disappointed at not having been able to meet up again. It had been twenty-one years since I met him. I was nine years old, and he would have been five. I'm sure he had a genuine reason for being unable to come. However, I can happily confirm that, in November 2023 — twenty-two years later — we managed to get our brother Ben to meet us at Collarenebri where our brother Bob lives. It was the best hug ever and to see the smile on his face and see the relief in his body language was the most heartwarming gift ever.

Unfortunately, my older brother Billy did not come along to the reunion we had in Dubbo either. Link-Up could not track him down because his whereabouts were unknown. None of us knew at the time that this would be the last opportunity for us to have met our brother Bill before he sadly passed away in April 2011. This news came as a huge shock to all of us, and we will always remember our brother Bill and keep him in our hearts forever.

None of us were able to attend Bill's funeral; however, his adoptive family did have a memorial service on a different day, which I was able to attend on behalf of our West family. The memorial service was held on Sunday 12 June 2011 at the Mylestom Surf Club in New South Wales (outside of Coffs Harbour). Bill's friends and family gathered to say their final farewells and scatter his ashes into the ocean. Bill was an avid surfer and a keen member of the Bellingen Valley North Beach Surf Club. Over the years Bill won many surf competitions and other trophies for his sporting abilities, such as swimming, cricket, and soccer.

I met Bill's mum, Mavis, his older sister, Carolyn, his sister-in-law, Donna, his cousins Emma, Kim, and Adam, and his niece, Kaitlyn. Bill's family not only opened their home, but also their hearts for all of Bill's birth family. When I arrived, they presented me with a photo album titled "William Wesley Barns ~ Bill Bowie ~ December 1970 – April 2011." On the opening page was a beautiful recent photo of Bill and the dedication read "To Joy and members of Bill's family, some of our special memories of our time together with 'Our Brother Bill' – 12 June 2011." Throughout the album were little loving notes that told a story of Bill's life from beginning to end. At the end of the album were photos taken at the crematorium on the day of his funeral. These photos included all his trophies and his prized possessions ~ his axe and his whisk. Bill trained as a chef in his younger years and always dreamed of owning his own restaurant. There was a photo of the lovely flowers that our sister Valerie sent on behalf of our family. Another photo was of a mosaic plaque made by a friend, Kia. This plaque is now in pride of place on the external wall of the Mylestom surf club, overlooking the ocean.

The morning of Bill's memorial service arrived, and it was absolutely pouring down with rain. Just the way I love it. His memorial service was well organised yet relaxed at the same time. In the rain, we gathered in a large circle around a specially prepared raft that was full of bunches of native flowers and foliage. We all held hands and Carolyn (Bill's sister) spoke and thanked everyone for their continued support and attendance. Carolyn acknowledged that despite being Bill's adoptive family, they were very aware that he also had a birth family that held him close in our hearts. It was a very touching moment, and on behalf of our West family, I deeply acknowledged and thanked them for their love and support that they had undoubtedly bestowed on Bill throughout his life. It was a very emotional and releasing moment for everyone.

At this point, a didgeridoo was being played and as we silently held hands, we said our final farewells to our brother Bill. After this, four of Bill's surfer mates carried the flower-laden raft and surfboard with the ashes through a guard of honour on the beach towards the awaiting ocean. We all followed them to the water's edge, where they set the raft down on the sand and then took Bill's ashes on surfboards out to his final place of rest, beyond where the waves crash, into the depths of the ocean. As each surfer individually battled the tide and the breakers, they finally reached the point of calm and formed a circle of honour where they could set Bill's spirit free. From the safety of the shore, we watched in awe as a whale in the distance blew her spout and a sea eagle glided silently, full of grace and dignity, above and seemingly beyond this world, into a sacred space. On the shore we knew that it was time to say our final farewells and each of us was encouraged to choose a flower from the raft and release it into the ocean, which was and always will be Billy's playground. With this, I was drawn to a native banksia that was red, black, and yellow in colour. It was a statement that I knew Bill would relate to. I took the flower and slowly walked to meet the sea. I pressed the flower to my lips and kissed it gently and waited for the ocean to wash in close. I then followed the tide out, not really wanting to let the flower go. Releasing it from my grasp, the tide took not only my flower, but also a part of my heart. With this flower, I sent all my love, hope, and fears, and in one sweep of the ocean, it was gone! Travel safe Bill, forever in our hearts, may you finally rest in peace!

We lost Bill in 2011, which was nine years after our big family reunion in Dubbo. Having now lost two brothers, it seemed even more important to stay in touch with the rest of my siblings and if I ever travelled to Sydney for work, I would ensure to catch up with my sister Beverley and her daughters Amanda and Janeen. My brother Bob dropped into Adelaide on one occasion with his work around 2004. Around 2010, I also visited my brother Bob, who'd moved to Canberra for a few years with his partner Louella. In 2012, after I lost my adoptive mum, my new partner of eight years and I travelled around Australia with our younger children Jay and Violet who were 8 and 6 years old. We ended up spending Christmas with my brother Mick and his family in Mackay, Queensland. That was super special and really gave me another opportunity to get to know my older brother a bit more. It was also a wonderful opportunity for Jay and Violet to meet their cousins Steven, Louise, and Ashleigh.

Another four years slipped by, with sporadic contact with my family, and life went on. Unexpectedly on 23 October 2016, I got a Facebook inbox message from my sister-in-law Linda. She wrote, "Hey Joy, have you seen this. Do you have a sister – Rosalind Margaret West. This young girl is looking for family and there were twelve kids, with a set of triplets and one being Ben. Micks just found it in Facebook, but we haven't contacted her. Reckon you're going to know more details." The minute I read that message I knew exactly who it was that was looking for my sister and I knew that the day had finally arrived to welcome my niece home. I couldn't contain my excitement and immediately, without too much thought, I sent my niece an inbox message. "Hello baby girl, I'm your mother's sister and I'm bawling my eyes out at this moment because I knew you were out there, and I've been waiting for this day sweety. I've got so much to tell you and lots of love to share. Welcome home." It took three hours of nail-biting before a response came: "Oh wow I can't believe it!" I sent her the photo of her mum, Rosalind, from when we had met at our very first Wollongong reunion. Her response was "Oh wow! Awesome! How beautiful, this is so beautiful! I can't wait to talk to you more and find out all about our family! It's so exciting and overwhelming and so special. I cannot believe it!"

From this initial contact our beautiful family wrapped around Rachel and embraced her into our West family. From the moment Rachel reached out to find us she has hit the family tracing tree running. She has a passion for knowledge and wanted to really document everything about our family and really capture our West family history.

I finally got to meet Rachel on 27 December 2016, it turned out perfectly as my brother Bob was visiting his daughter Shona, who lived in Dubbo, New South Wales, which was near where Rachel was living in Orange, New South Wales, so we all caught up together. The rest is history. Rachel has been actively bringing us all back together for reunions from the moment she met us. She helped plan another big reunion in Sydney 2017. It was even more special than our Dubbo reunion. This time we were feeling more comfortable with each other and could really enjoy just being a family having fun together. It was so good just allowing our kids to get to know each other.

The next family reunion was recently held in 2024 and was planned by NSW Link-Up on behalf of our brother David who hadn't yet met Mick, Bob, Jordie, Ben, Olive or me. He has met our sister Valerie, whom he grew up with some of the time and our sister Beverley whom he met when they were older.

David — what a kind-hearted, beautiful soul. He's our oldest living brother. I met him in Walgett in September 2024. He travelled from Sydney with the NSW Link-Up workers and our sister Valerie. Rachel travelled down from

Queensland, and my daughter Violet and I travelled up from South Australia, and our brother Bob isn't far from Walgett. I had literally been driving for two days, and we pulled into Walgett not long after David and the mob had arrived. I pulled up in the car park of the motel and realised that David was right there. I saw my big sister Valerie waiting in the background and knew it was time to go and meet my biggest brother. It was such a beautiful hug. I'm sure my niece Rachel captured the moment with lots of clicks of the camera.

Later that night, I got to sit outside the motel room and have a bit more of a yarn with my big brother. He was so laid back. Even though he looked most like Bob, his nature was quite different from my other brothers. He seemed calmer and more introverted. His humour is very dry but very witty. I just loved him straight away. He was hungry for knowledge about our family and really didn't know that much, so it was a great opportunity to share what I knew without overwhelming him too much.

The next day, our brother Bob came to Walgett to meet David. I can tell you there wasn't a dry eye as those two blokes hugged. I knew David felt connected to me but to hug a brother was a whole new level of connection and it showed. That day we took our brother out to the cemetery to where our beautiful mum Joan was buried and introduced our brother to our mother. We had a female Aboriginal Elder, whom we called Aunty out of respect, come out and hold a special welcoming smoking ceremony for our brother David. It was very powerful. She spoke in our traditional Gamilaraay language and welcomed David home. Then we went on an adventure through the local area and visited houses and places where we knew that our mum had lived and been to. We found some cousins who also said hello and told him what they remembered of our mum. It filled all our spiritual cups to be back on Country and meeting our mob.

That night our brother Bob invited us to go back to his place. David was happy to join us, and he sat in the front seat of my car. I'd never felt prouder to be a chauffeur for my big brother. That night Violet, Bob, and I took a dip in the local heated bore water swimming pool. It was amazing. After we'd showered, we went to the local pub for dinner. It was a Friday night, and all the locals were there — mostly Bob's drinking mates. He was proud as punch to introduce both David and me to his mates: "This is my brother and sister." We shared an Aussie pub meal and then the boys played a game of 8-ball pool with some locals. The smallest and most simple things, such as that, nearly burst my heart with joy and pride to see my brothers being brothers, doing brotherly things. That's what we'd been missing our whole lives. Just hanging out together, laughing, teasing and protecting each other. It was, and always will be, a priceless memory. As the night ended and all the photos were taken Bob and David embraced, you could hear their big hands slapping each other's backs, then they were both struggling to hold back their sobs. But men being men, this didn't last long before they pulled themselves together. However, the memory and feeling that sight brought up for me will forever remind me of what we've lost, but also of what we've gained.

Chapter 4
Footprints Across the Land

As a child, we moved to seven different townships. Australia is a big place, and it is made up of six States and two Territories. I have lived in three of those States and the only State that I have not travelled to is Western Australia. I feel very blessed to have been given the opportunity to have seen so much of Australia. I'm sure most people would find moving around very unsettling; however, I quite enjoyed the adventure. I don't think it did me any harm. I think it improved my communication skills and helped to boost my self-confidence and self-esteem. It was a matter of necessity to develop these communication skills, or I wouldn't have had any friends. I love people and I love making friends. It's fun finding out everything about different people and their lives. It is so revealing to see where people have come from and hear about their experiences, dramas and dreams. As a kid, I never questioned why we moved so much. I simply thought it was because my parents found it hard to find enough work in small townships. Little did I know that there was a more insidious explanation that was openly revealed once I turned fifteen. Remember the scandalous affair that must have raised a few too many enquiring eyebrows. These days no one even cares, but back then my mum was paranoid about gossip. Who she thought they were going to tell and what she thought they would say, I have no idea. It must have been quite exhausting living in such fear. The first place we lived at was in a tiny place near Port Macquarie, New South Wales, called

Pappinbarra. My adoptive parents built their first home in Australia there and I have vague memories of this property. It has stayed close to the family as my parents' best friends bought it in 1975, however a few years ago they sold it and moved into town. Years of blood, sweat, and tears went into renovating the home and the gardens and both were breathtakingly amazing. There is a creek running behind the house and I remember being taken down there for a swim and a splash. It's only now that I realise it's situated in rainforest country, and the river is full of leeches. I'm not sure if I'd be happy swimming there now with this knowledge. The one distinct thing I can remember about Pappinbarra is the sound of the local bellbirds. It is a very distinct sound, and one that always tells me where I am. I feel like I have come home when I hear that sound. Close to Pappinbarra is another town called Wauchope (pronounced war-hope). This is the place where I just loved to go as a kid, because my parents would take me to my two most favourite childhood places in the universe. The first was called "Fantasy Glades" and the other was called "Timbertown." In those days, Fantasy Glades would have been the cream of the crop of theme parks. It was fantastic! It was owned and set up by little people in 1968. I reckon that's why so many children loved it, and everything was just the right size for a child. I remember Snow White and the Seven Dwarfs' little cottage. It even had all the seven beds lined up in a neat row upstairs with patchwork quilts laid out. It was amazing. I loved that place. I have so many fond memories of it — it was magical. It was in operation for thirty-five years bringing childhood stories to life, but sadly now it has been left for nature to swallow up. Timbertown was the next place we used to visit every school holidays. Timbertown was set out as an entire township of colonial pioneers. There were blacksmith shops, horses and carts carrying supplies, and bullock teams pulling heavy loads of timber through the streets. All the staff at Timbertown were wearing olden-day clothes and you could smell the fresh sawdust from the operating sawmill. The concept of Timbertown began in 1970 and the plan was to recreate a working timber settlement from 1880 to 1910. Work began in 1973 on the creation of Timbertown and three years later it opened in 1976, and it must have been impressive in its day. As a child I had no understanding of Australia's black history, so my childhood ignorance enabled me to just soak up the atmosphere of the hustle and bustle of what simply seemed like an olden-day town. Now I am almost ashamed to say that I loved this trip down colonialism lane, but it was a big part of my childhood experience that I cannot and do not want to forget. Unfortunately, my other favourite childhood theme park, Fantasy Glades is no more; luckily, Timbertown has survived the times. To be honest, I think the bigger "theme parks" of Queensland have taken their place. The next place we moved to was Tottenham. It is right in the centre of New South Wales, and I was four years old when we moved there. I remember I started kindergarten at Tottenham, and I have photos of me sitting on the front veranda hugging my best friend Leonie and her brother Lesley. They were both white kids, but I didn't notice the difference, and they didn't care. We were like three peas in a pod. I feel like I was always off on an adventure somewhere with them. I know it can't have been far from home, because I was too young to be roaming all over the countryside. I do remember one of our favourite treats Leonie taught me to concoct: take a glass; put four huge scoops of "Sunshine" powder milk into it; followed this with two scoops of "Milo;" then followed by just enough water to make a paste. Mix it all together like there's no tomorrow and hey presto; you've just created the most delicious concoction that you'll ever taste. We loved it! You could always tell when we had been sneaking in the kitchen to get another cupful. The Milo ring around our mouths was always a dead giveaway. While in Tottenham we lived in two different houses. The first one was basic single-storey house, but then my parents trucked in a second house which was put up on stilts on the vacant block next door to our first house. I remember the huge semi-trailer truck delivering it, and somehow they jacked it up onto the stilts. It was the most magnificent home that I remember us ever having. I would love to own it today. I often wonder if it is still standing. It had a huge veranda that wrapped around two sides of the house, and it was on that veranda that I learnt to ride my first bike. I remember the Christmas when "Santa" brought me my first big bike. I woke up on Christmas morning and went into the lounge room to find my new bike hidden under a sheet. It was sky blue and had a long white saddle seat splashed with a colourful flower power design. At the back of the bike, there was a long arched bar that my dad used to hold onto while running behind me to get me started! I loved that bike, and I loved my dad for teaching me to ride it. It was the best present! My dad also built me my first cubby house in Tottenham. This is the only cubby house I had that was on the ground; all my future cubby houses were up in a tree. I was so lucky! Pallamallawa was the next place we moved to, when I was six years old, it was thirty kilometres east of Moree, which was remarkably close to where I was born. It was a small country town in the north-west of New South Wales. It is lovingly known as Pally by the locals. I only realised later in life that it is right smack bang in the middle of my mother's Kamilaroi country. I also only recently realised that my older brothers, Mick, and Bob, were living in Collarenebri and Warialda, which is one to two hours from

Pallamallawa and the triplets were living in separate small towns close by too. It's amazing and sad that we were all so close, yet so far away from each other. In Pally, we lived in a small house on a hill at the top end of a large property. The property owners must have been a sorghum (grain food for animals) farmer because I remember the big storage sheds being full of sorghum. I was invited to go and play at the property owner's place with the farmer's kids. The house looked like something out of the film "Gone with the Wind." The halls were long and endless, and the doors were huge. The kids had a playroom filled with toys and there were lovely bunches of deliciously fragrant wisteria growing and hanging off the pergola out the front of the big columned entrance. I didn't often get to play with those kids, but I can still remember their house and the beautiful smell of the wisteria, and I distinctly remember the large black-and-white mosaic-tiled floors. It's funny what things we remember from our childhood and how different smells evoke different memories. Pally was the place where I baked my first batch of mud pies. Mum gave me an old cardboard box, which I promptly turned on its side and balanced up against the outside wall of the house. It was a lovely warm day, perfect for baking. I mixed up a nice batch of mud and was covered right up to my elbows with it. Add a pinch of sand; a handful of dry grass; two handfuls of dirt and add two cups of water. Mix, mix, and mix with a stick and — hey presto — you have the perfect mud pie mixture. Now the fun begins and it's time to get the hands real dirty. Take one handful of mud, roll it into a firm ball, then promptly squash between your palms and slap it onto a stolen tray from your mum's kitchen cupboard. Oops sorry mum! Place tray with mud pie patties in the makeshift cardboard-box oven and close fake doors and leave half the day to bake in the sun. Perfect! I don't think

I've ever cooked anything of that fine standard since. We weren't in that house too long when it was time to move again. This time we didn't move far, we just moved down the hill to the bottom of the property. It was a bigger house, and it was the first one where I had a bedroom of my own. It came off my mum and dad's bedroom via French doors, and it was an enclosed part of the veranda. There was also a door that went straight out onto the veranda. I don't think I spent one whole night sleeping in that bedroom because I was petrified of the dark. One night mum and dad put me to bed, and I could not settle because I was absolutely convinced that there was a big brown bear right outside my window. Dad went outside with a torch and searched high and low for that "non-existent" bear, and I still ended up sleeping in a spare bed right next to my mum and dad's bed. I remember stretching my little arm out and falling asleep holding my mum's hand. Its memories like these that will live with me forever. Our next move was to Queensland and this time we lived on a humungous cattle and sheep station called "Curry Curry" outside of St George. St George is an outback rural town five hundred kilometres inland from Brisbane in the southern part of Queensland. It was a hot and very dry place. I was only seven years old when I used to catch the school bus for an hour each way to get to and from school. I distinctly remember my bedroom at this place because mum had made me "Snow White and the Seven Dwarfs" curtains she hung up in my bedroom. I don't know whether it was me who was fascinated with Snow White, or whether it was mum, but I also remember that for a fancy-dress party I did go as Snow White, which looking back is just so insane that it's laughable. I was as different from Snow White as day is from night. Yet somehow, I ended up finding myself in the full fancy dress costume my mum and dad had painstakingly created just for me. My dad was an exceptionally good artist, and he hand-drew a picture of each of the seven dwarfs on my flowing yellow skirt. I cannot remember much more about it, but I am intrigued when I look back. Was it me wishing I was white, or was it simply me fulfilling my childhood fantasy of being a princess, who happened to be white? Perhaps my trips to Fantasy Glades gave me the inspiration. I was a bit too young to think about my cultural identity, but upon reflection these were the early rumblings of my cultural dissonance — being torn between two worlds. We weren't at "Curry Curry" for more than a year before we moved into the township of St George. This was the house where my dad built me my first tree house. There was a huge Eucalyptus gum tree in our backyard, and it would need four adults with their arms interlocked to reach around its girth. Based on this measurement, I estimate that the tree was about four hundred years old. This tree was a perfect foundation for the floor of my cubby house, which sat nicely in the fork of the tree. Dad nailed in the floor and then attached about six wooden steps to the trunk for me to climb up to get onto the platform of the cubby house, which was about two metres off the ground. I loved it. It didn't have a roof; it just had the platform and a little benchtop on one side. I remember climbing up there and taking a bag full of army supplies I got from goodness knows where. I'd sit up there, just sucking on tubes of sweetened condensed milk. I am surprised I have any teeth left because of the amount of sugar I consumed during my childhood. We were only in St George long enough to make friends with the local neighbours before it was time to move on again. This time we moved back to New South Wales, and it was a real adventure. My parents decided to take on a completely new occupation, and they became the caretakers of a caravan park in a little country "goldmining" town called Nundle. This little historic town is less than an hour's drive south-east of Tamworth, the country music capital of Australia. I loved Nundle. We moved there when I was 9 years old, and it was in this town that I started to form the happy memories of my childhood adventures. It was a safe place, and I was able to explore the countryside without a worry in the world. We lived in two caravans joined together in the middle by an annexe. I didn't think it was strange in any way that our home was made up of caravans, and our bathroom was the shared amenities block of the caravan park. It was all completely normal to me. I loved the buzz of the caravan park, particularly during school holidays. There were always regular holidaymakers who would come back every year with their families, and I loved catching up with all of their kids. I was never bored and always had something to do or somewhere to go and explore. We lived right in the middle of the township, and the caravan park was on the banks of the local Peel River — a local hot spot for gold panning. My uncle taught me how to gold pan, and I loved it. We would put on our gumboots, grab our gold pans, shovels, picks, and head down to the river. We'd find a spot that looked as though no one had explored it before, and we'd start digging around the roots of a tree, thinking that a big nugget of gold had lodged in the roots in years gone by. We'd take a shovelful of dirt and dump it into the sifter balanced on top of the gold pan. We'd shake it from side-to-side watching the small bits of dirt drop through to the gold pan below, leaving the larger stuff in the sift. We'd check for nuggets, which were very rare if not near impossible to find, and then it was time to work just with the gold pan. It was such a relaxing pastime — almost hypnotic. Swish, swish, swish — I would roll the gold pan around in a circular motion releasing the remaining dirt back into the river from where it had come. I always made sure to check the rim of the gold pan for any small specks of gold that I could pick up with my little fingers and put into a thin, clear jar filled with water. It was so much fun, and my eyes were as sharp as eagles, looking for those tiny gold flecks. I loved the feel of the water gurgling past my gumboots, and I can still see the willow trees draping in the water and blowing in the breeze. I loved gold panning, and I miss doing it. It was pure magic. Whenever I'd get hungry, I'd leave Uncle to the gold panning and go and pick two mouthfuls of wild blackberries on the riverbanks. With fingers stained and my belly aching, I'd go home at the end of a fun-filled day to a lovely home-cooked stew. Life was so simple then! I could have just lived in that time zone forever. I have fond memories of Nundle, and it was sad to move on again. We left Nundle and moved to the other side of Tamworth, to a small town called Moonbi, which had a large mountain called the Moonbi Range, which was part of the Great Dividing Range in the Northern Tablelands of New South Wales. I have no idea why we moved there. Maybe it had something to do with the big fight my mum, dad and uncle had, when I remember seeing my mum punch my dad in the nose. As you may remember my mum hated gossip, so it was easier to leave Nundle than stay and face the nosey parker glares. I missed the lifestyle of Nundle, but I was used to change. Our new house was huge. It had seven bedrooms, and it seemed to stretch for miles from one end of the house to the other. It also had a little creek running through the back of the property and I used to take my little blow-up air mattress to the top of the creek and float my way downstream. I'd then turn around and trudge my way back up stream just to repeatedly do it all over again. It was fun. These were the years when I first started to feel like a real teenager. I was all of 11 years old, and I wanted to sleep over at girlfriend's houses; I was interested in make-up;

went to school discos and started to spend hours looking in the mirror. What a laugh! We weren't at Moonbi for long, perhaps a year and it was time to move again. This time it was a more significant move to another state in a little country town in Queensland called Proston. It was eight hours drive away from Moonbi, so I wasn't happy about this move, because it was too far away for my friends to visit, but I had no choice and resentfully had to move. I am so glad I didn't get my own way back then because this turned out to be the best move of my whole life. I loved our new lifestyle. It was simply perfect! We lived about an hour's drive out of the township of Proston on a huge one-hundred-acre block of natural bush land. There was no house, no power, no phone, and no running water. We were completely isolated, and I thought that my parents were crazy, but this was where I spent the best years of my teenage life. My dad, mum and uncle built our house from scratch. They got the trees bulldozed to clear a spot to put the house on. In the meantime, we lived in a caravan and tent. It didn't seem long at all before my dad had laid down a slab of concrete and put up the small beginnings of a log cabin that soon developed into our beautiful home. Our whole house was made from what was known as "hog backs." These were off cuts of timber from one of the small local sawmills. The house had four bedrooms and two bathrooms, one inside and the other outside. Our home was built in stages. From week-to-week or month-to-month, as we could afford the building materials, another room or two would be added. I remember my bedroom was huge. It was the largest bedroom I've ever had in my whole life. Mum painted it my favourite colour, lilac. I was so spoiled! We had a wood stove oven to heat the hot water, and we used a generator for electricity. We had solar power panels for some of the essentials like lights at night when we didn't need the generator on. Our little black and white television used to get hooked up to a car battery sitting on the kitchen floor so I could watch all my favourite TV shows, like "Neighbours" and "Home and Away." We used the gas stovetop if we just wanted to boil the kettle, and it had a whistle on it like a steam train. Mum used to iron our clothes with a heavy old wrought iron she would warm up right on the wood stove hot plates. Mum would wash the clothes with an old wringer washing machine and sewed our clothes with her old foot pedal-operated treadle sewing machine. I remember that mum accidentally ran that treadle needle right over her finger and the needle snapped right off in her finger. I almost fainted when she showed me. I remember that my uncle got a pair of pliers and just pulled it out of her finger. Gee they bred em tough back in those days. I can still see the big old kerosene fridge whose door mum painted sky blue as if to make it feel more modern even though it was antique and made in the 1920's. We had the biggest veggie patch that you've ever seen. In a city it would be classified as a market garden. We had chooks and ducks in a chicken pen, because mum has a phobia of birds, and she would faint if they came too close. We even had a pig for a short while. I don't even want to imagine where he mysteriously disappeared to. I'm sure we had pork chops for dinner that night. I started Year 7 at Proston State School it was an hour's journey from home on the local school bus. The town kids knew us as 'Prickle Farmers." Everyone in town thought that we weren't real farmers; we were just hobby farmers and therefore could only grow prickles. Who would have thought that there would be snobbery amongst farmers? I loved that bus ride to school every day. It was a social occasion. We all had our own seats in the bus, and we all knew the drill of who was to get dropped off where and when. It wouldn't have mattered if the bus driver got sick and couldn't drive because, by that stage, all of us on the bus knew how to drive anyway. I remember one afternoon Mum and Dad took me into Kingaroy, which was the next biggest town to where we lived, to look at a pony. His name was Pilot, and it was love at first sight for me. When Pilot came home to our property, I don't think he knew what he'd be in for, but we certainly shared three years of fun times together. If a horse could laugh, I'm sure he would have been laughing at me learning to ride. When we first got Pilot, we only had his halter and his bridle — no saddle. Now remember me and patience aren't good friends and I'm sure it will be a lifelong skill that I keep working to develop. As a kid, I was even less patient than I am now, and, being a big shot, I just couldn't wait until we got a saddle. So off I went, bare back. I thought at first, I'd just start at a walking pace, but what sort of fun is there to that? It's not dangerous enough! Once I got the balance thing happening, I'd give Pilot a nudge with my heels, and we'd start trotting. Well, what a bumpy ride! I'd slide from one side of his fat belly to the other, but somehow, I managed to stay on. Still not satisfied with that, I upped the pace a bit and he broke into a canter. Too scared to really kick Pilot, I'd pull back on the reins, and he'd go back to trotting so fast and I'd be bumping so much that I thought I'd never stay on. Then, suddenly, he'd break into a smooth canter again and stretch his stumpy legs out and for a split second I'd just slump down and relax and enjoy the comfortable ride and the ease of his strides. It was magic. However, the problem arose when we had to slow from the smooth canter back to a trot while trying to manoeuvre a corner. This was not a good combination for a bareback learner and yes, off I'd come with a hard thump to the ground. It wasn't so much the falling off that was the problem, it was more the point that if I fell off, Pilot would always trot off about a dozen steps in front of me and make me walk all the way home trying to catch him. No wonder I was so skinny and nicknamed "Bones" back then! My best friends out on Glencoe Road were Kim and Jodie. They lived at "Trinity 13" about a five-minute drive from where I lived at "Kantagri" which is pronounced "Can't Agree". I remember my parents and uncle used to argue about everything and certainly couldn't agree on many things. So, this property was appropriately named. I loved our place, but I was the only child at home by this stage and would quickly get bored with my own company. Every weekend, without fail, I would look to go to Kim and Jodie's place. Mum would pull her hair out and wonder why I didn't want to stay at home, but I couldn't help but follow the action. At Kim and Jodie's there was always something to do and mischief to get up to. I would usually saddle up my horse and set off at eight o'clock every Saturday morning. I would get to their place and put my horse "Pilot" in their home paddock and look forward to whatever we were doing for the weekend. Usually, it involved work, like walking behind a four-wheel drive (4WD) and trailer and chucking all the tree roots and large sticks and stumps that were in the ploughed paddock into the trailer, this was known as stick picking. We branded cows, built stockyards, fixed fences, went motor bike riding or mustered cattle. We'd jump in the old beat up 4WD Land Cruiser with about three big dogs in the back, all dripping their sweaty tongues right on my head and farting stinkily all the way around the huge property. I cringe when I think about it now, but at the time I wouldn't have wanted to be at any other place in the whole world. I remember one time when Kim, Jodie and I were all bored. Despite having a huge dam to swim in, motorbikes and horses to ride, we were still bored. Kim's big brother Robert who loved motorbikes, had what he thought was a clever idea. He decided he would tow us on our pushbikes all the way round their thousand-acre block. The only problem was there was only one motorbike and three girls. Problem solved! Robert tied a chain of three push bikes to each other and then tied the end to his motorbike. Oh, my goodness what a recipe for disaster. Off we set, just like a semi-trailer truck — commonly known as a road train in Queensland. Around the dirt tracks we were being towed with Robert leading the way with his motorbike, pulling Jodie, then Kim and then me on our "deadly treadleys" — pushbikes. I don't know how we didn't kill ourselves, but I know we all had fun. This is a serious warning to any daredevils reading this: please don't ever try this, we were insane! The years spent at "Kantagri" were some of the best years of my life. As I reflect on that time of my life, I know I was lucky to have spent those years growing up there. Mum and dad were not rich people, but they were hard workers. They worked for every cent they ever earned, and that money was put back into the family home to make our lives a little more comfortable and enjoyable. My life was so good and like any other self-absorbed teenager, I was so busy, I didn't even notice or suspect that the separation of my mum and dad was coming. I'm sure dad didn't even know it was going to happen either. I was so engrossed in high school, my friends, my horse, and myself that I was unaware my entire world was about to be turned upside down. I wouldn't say there could ever be a suitable time in a child's life for parents to decide they are going to go their separate ways. I distinctly remember it was a decision I was not openly or wholly involved in making, nor should I have been. I just remember that one day, on the way back from town with Mum and Uncle, Uncle pulled over the car and Mum said to me, "I'm going to leave your father, and Uncle I will be living together as man and wife, do you want to come with us or live with your father?" Suddenly, I felt like the life was being sucked right out of me. As if I was in a vacuum, and I felt like I was crawling in one direction but being pulled in another direction at the same time. I was torn between doing what I felt was right and I should have done versus doing what my heart was telling me and what I wanted to do. It was the biggest decision I had to make in my whole young life. I knew I couldn't share this burden with anyone, so after thinking about it endlessly overnight, I came to a decision that completely changed the direction of my life. I chose to move to Adelaide with mum and uncle. Begrudgingly, I had to lie to Dad initially and give him the impression that we were living in Darwin, which is in the Northern Territory, instead of telling him the truth that we were in South Australia. This was because Mum and Uncle were afraid, that Dad would follow Mum. Dad did have a shotgun on the farm, and I have no doubt that he was so angry that he may well have wanted to use it. Thankfully that didn't happen and after about three months, the truth was revealed, and dad understood why I had been told to deceive him and for this I was terribly sorry, but I feel that it was out of my control and I'm sure dad forgave me and understood the predicament that I'd been placed in. I was fifteen years old when we moved away from Proston, Queensland, to Elizabeth, South Australia. If you thought the last move was a big one, this one took twenty-two hours to drive. Everything that brought me pleasure and a sense of security was left behind, my dad, my home, my friends, my school, my community, and most of all, my horse and my dogs. Once again, I found myself enrolled in yet another school. This time it was Elizabeth High School. I didn't know anyone, and I had to make new friends all over again. I missed dad terribly and I especially missed all my old friends. At first, my friends wrote to me religiously, but slowly as the months went on, we all just got too busy with the demands of high school and teenage life, and, a bit like my relationship with my sister Rosalind, we just grew apart. My new life was worlds apart from the life I had led in the small country towns I had grown up in. Adelaide was the first city I had ever lived in, and as a curious teenager with older parents, I used every opportunity to celebrate this newfound freedom. After my first week at Elizabeth High, I was taken under the wing of a girl whose name was Kylie. I was so thankful for Kylie's friendship. The first weekend Kylie made a point to come to my place and asked if I would like to go with her to the local swimming pool, known as the Aquadome. This is a huge undercover indoor swimming pool with an outdoor pool, which was used as a diving pool. Thankfully, after much begging, Mum agreed for me to go with Kylie, and it was from there that my network of friends began to grow. Thank you, Kylie. You will never know the gratitude I felt for your friendship at that time. Within a month of staying with the people we'd been lodging with, mum and uncle found a rental property in one of the northern suburbs, which used to be called Elizabeth West and is now known as Davoren Park. It didn't take too long before I had a nice little group of friends I'd regularly hang out with after school and on the weekends. I felt like I really fitted in. I must admit, fashion had never really played a significant role in my life, but now in this big new school it was of utmost importance. I remember the first day I turned up to high school in a white and sky-blue polka dot t-shirt and a sports skirt. The country bumpkin in me thought I looked great, but I quickly realised the city chicks thought it was so not cool! When we first arrived in South Australia, my closet was empty, but thankfully mum and uncle started doing voluntary work at St Vincent De Paul and mum worked out the back sorting all the donated clothes. Mum would get first pick of all the amazing, trendy clothes that perfectly matched my teenager needs and desires. I was always thrilled with the clothes I'd manage to mix and match and the new fashion statements I'd make. My crazy clothes, plus a large array of way out-there shoes and shorts, were two of the things that I was renowned for at high school. It was at Elizabeth High that I really started to become aware of my Aboriginality. Whenever I met any new kids or teachers, they always asked me, "What nationality are you?" This was a question that had never really struck me before, and over the years I had been protected by the small country towns where my adoptive family lived, where everyone knew my family and me and hence no one ever asked me this question. I was always proud to say that I was "part" Aboriginal. I now know that my answer was totally inappropriate and offensive, and the other "Nunga" kids — a South Australian word for Aboriginal — quickly threw back at me; "So which part of ya is black?" They'd all started laughing at me, so I quickly learnt that in no uncertain terms, "Ya either black or ya not, ya can't be part." Nowadays when I hear this same declaration by someone else, I want to say to them "So which part of you is offended when I say you're either black or you're not, what's it gonna be?" Instead, I just bite my tongue and think I was young once too, and they are obviously still on their own identity journey. I was so naive back then. I didn't even know that Aboriginal people from New South Wales and Victoria called themselves "Kooris" and each of the Australian states and territories had their own names; for example, people from Western Australia are known as "Noongas", and Queensland Aboriginal people call themselves "Murris". When we moved, I am sure that my family didn't know that Elizabeth was one of the lowest socio-economic suburbs in Adelaide. It was also one of the suburbs with the highest population of Aboriginal families. This resulted in high numbers of Aboriginal students in the school that I had enrolled. About fifty Aboriginal students, from Reception to Year 12, were enrolled at Kaurna Plains School in 1987, which was just on the other side of the Elizabeth High school oval and had only been open for one year. It was also one of the first Aboriginal schools for both primary and secondary Aboriginal students in South Australia and certainly not something that I'd ever come across. The principal asked Mum, "Would Joy like to enrol at Kaurna Plains School with the other Aboriginal kids?" I was horrified and quickly said "No, that's okay. I'll just go here to Elizabeth High." It was obvious that I feared my own people. This was all new and foreign to me because throughout my primary school years, I had attended schools where there were no other Aboriginal kids at all. Now suddenly, I was attending a school that had heaps of Aboriginal kids. For the first time I felt different from everyone, I felt like a real outcast. Which made no sense, because I thought it was what I had yearned for my whole life. But once confronted with the reality of it, I felt so alone and frightened of my own identity. It didn't take long before I started to embrace my Aboriginality, and I started to feel that sense of connection with the kids and with my Aboriginal culture. It was exactly what I'd been searching for my whole life. I was always amazed at how these Aboriginal kids always seemed to have heaps of friends. It was only later that I realised that most of their friends were, in fact, their brothers, sisters, or cousins, who were also considered brothers and sisters, and whom they'd grown up with. Unfortunately, I had come to South Australia as an only child, and I was adopted, I was like an orphan compared to them. Apart from knowing that I was Aboriginal, that was where the similarities ended, because I could not answer their questions about my Aboriginal family. I now know these kids were just trying to find out who I was, where was I from and who was I related to. Little did they know that this was going to be nearly impossible to find out, because, at that stage, not even I knew who my own mob was! Over the three years of high school, I gradually gained acceptance amongst the Nunga kids and became well known within the Aboriginal community. I put this acceptance down to one of the things I had in common with the other Aboriginal students — a talent for athletics. When sports day came, I was the one that took home all the blue first place ribbons. I was the fastest female runner in all the events in my year level at the school. On school sports day, about twenty of the Nunga kids would come over from Kaurna Plains School and stand on the Kaurna Plains side of the oval, cheering me on to win. It wasn't until later in life that I came to realise a win for me also meant a win for them. It was a celebration of another blackfulla's victory, and it was something to be proud of and equally shared. After being at the school for a year, I soon realised that there were boys out there. During the summer months, my friends Mandy, Naomi, Joanne, and I would spend our weekends swimming at the Elizabeth Aquadome. We would get there from the minute it opened and stay all day until it shut. During this time, hours of sunbaking and spectating took place. Once again, I was different from the Nunga girls. I was brought up to be proud of my body and wasn't embarrassed to just wear my bathers without a big T-shirt over the top. The other Nunga girls would wear bike pants and T-shirts to their knees and be very embarrassed or "shame" about their bodies. I was unfamiliar with the word "shame." I had never been embarrassed or self-conscious of my body, but, looking at how those Nunga girls were behaving and the disgusted looks they were giving me, I soon took on their "shame" behaviours just to try and fit in. These days, I'm not so proud of my body and I now share those feelings of wanting to hide beneath my clothes. I know that this wasn't the same reason these girls were shame about parading their bodies as teenagers. It was more of a protective behaviour so as not to bring unwanted attention to yourself, it just wasn't done. Perhaps this was also learnt behaviour from mission or institution days, passed down the generations to protect young Aboriginal women from roaming station owners' eyes and filthy hands. My first love at high school was an Aboriginal boy. He lived in the same area as me before I moved to Salisbury North. I can't remember the exact way that we ended up together, but undoubtedly it would have been through endless pushing and influence by my girlfriends. We stayed together on and off for a year and I remember he left high school in year eleven while I stayed on to complete year twelve. During this time, he moved to Parafield Gardens, which was a bit closer for me to ride my bike from Salisbury North to meet him. It still took me a good hour to ride there, but I was infatuated and would have ridden to the end of the earth, had my mum let me. Looking back now, I know that my relationship with this Aboriginal boy was a safe attempt of me exploring my Aboriginality and trying to work out and find out more about my identity. This Aboriginal boy and his family taught me so much about being "black", and I learnt so much about who I was and about my culture, I thank his family for opening their home and inviting me into another side of life, which at the time, was very unfamiliar and overwhelming to me. During this period of my life, white boys were of no interest to me, and I was attracted to Aboriginal boys. I reckon I was as intriguing to them as they were to me. However, at the beginning of Year Twelve, a certain English boy by the name of Rusty (pseudo) started to pay a bit of extra attention to me. Unbeknown to me at the time, he would turn out to be my future husband and the father of my son Jordan. Rusty started at Elizabeth High School around the same time as I did. Rusty and his family had emigrated from England, so he, too, was new to the school. Apparently, Rusty noticed me on my first day of school, but it took a while to pluck up the courage to approach me —or, should I say pester me. Mysteriously, Rusty managed to work out which classes I was in, and he'd end up in the same lessons as me. In the beginning, I just used to think he was nice, but very annoying. After weeks of pestering, I agreed to go out with him on a date to a football match. The local South Australian National Football League (SANFL) team, "Centrals", was playing at Football Park. Rusty was exceptionally smooth and even had his driver's licence while still at school. He picked me up with my two other girlfriends in his parents' car and that was the start of a twelve-year relationship. Rusty was everything that my parents wanted for their daughter. Rusty and I shared years of fantastic times together. We both worked part-time throughout school to save enough money so that we could travel up to Queensland to visit my adoptive dad, Fen. I really don't know how we managed to do all the things we did on the tight budget we had, but we survived and enjoyed our adventures. After we left school (Rusty failing and me entering university) we decided it was time to stop living between our parents' houses, so we went looking for a small flat to move into. We found a nice two-bedroom, second-storey flat in Salisbury. We only paid eighty dollars per week, can you believe that, and it was just what we needed while we were on a tight budget, with me being a first-year university student and Rusty just starting his apprenticeship as a chef. I look back and say to myself, those were the good old days, minimal worries, and maximum fun. Despite these being tough financial times, they made me a stronger and a more self-determined person. I had to develop time management skills, study full-time, work part-time, and made sure the bills were paid, just to keep a roof over our heads. From the minute we moved out of home, we never expected or asked for any financial help from our parents or anyone else. We were only eighteen years old, and I look around at today's teenage population and think about our achievement at such an early age. Not many kids can or want to do what we did back then. I know the way we managed was due to both sets of our parents having instilled in us strong work ethics and values through setting good examples and being good role models. Moving out of home, starting my Bachelor of Applied Science at university, and having to work part-time really marked a new era. I was officially an adult!

Chapter 5
Three Degrees of Separation

I don't particularly remember saying that I really wanted to go to university, and I certainly wasn't working towards it during high school. So how I ended up enrolled there is a bit of a mystery to me. But I wouldn't have changed it for the world. As is the case with most kids, I didn't really have any idea of what I wanted to do after I finished high school. I did do work experience in an administrative position, as a secretary at a doctor's surgery, but other than that, I really didn't know what else there was out there for me.

I remember I had an appointment with the student counsellor, and we discussed my options. It must just have been something I said about my love for the environment that triggered an idea for the counsellor. The next thing I knew, she was talking to me about studying at university and becoming a qualified park ranger. This all sounded exciting to me and all these images of cuddling koalas, wearing a uniform, and driving a 4WD started to form in my mind. With these pictures strongly embedded in my imagination, I was happy to go along with the flow of things and the ball started to roll. Before I knew it, I had been accepted into the University of South Australia, which back then was known as the College of Advanced Technology and Education, and began my studies in Conservation and Park Management at the Salisbury Campus.

I studied for the next three years of my life, followed by a further two and a half years of postgraduate studies. I now have my Bachelor of Applied Science (Conservation and Park Management) and my Graduate Diploma in Education (Secondary), and a Masters in Social Science (Counselling), which was another two years of study. Those years at the Salisbury Campus were the hardest, yet best years of my life. I look back and think, "Did I really do that?" Then I say to myself, "Yeah, I did do that, but I have no bloody idea how!" It is amazing what you can achieve when you finally set your mind to it. I made lifelong, fantastic friends during this time. All the subjects were compulsory and, because our year-level group was not that large, we were constantly together in all our classes. We were just like one big happy family who had to put up with each other for three years straight.

Around the Salisbury campus, we were known as "The Parkies" and if you were a Parkie, then you had to look the part. So, during those years, I wore khaki army pants and walking boots and looked crusty all the time. It was absolute bliss because you didn't really have to dress up, no one cared how you looked, and you fitted in just fine with everyone else. I miss those carefree days. I know that when I first started at university, I was young, fresh out of school, and very naive. The group of students were a mixture of school leavers and mature-age students. This made for a nice blend, and I learnt lessons about growing up, being responsible and maturing from the older students. It worked quite well, and there never really seemed to be a distinction made between our ages. I felt there was a level playing field since the whole university experience was new to all of us.

When I started at university, there were two other male Aboriginal students in my year level. They were also from interstate. Their names were Ken and Ricky. Ken was a school leaver from Queensland, and Ricky was older than us. He was originally from New South Wales but lived in Queensland.

Having Ken and Rick there alongside me was a real help and support. In the end, Ken and I were the only two Aboriginal students that graduated in our year level. In fact, we were the second and third Aboriginal students to graduate with that degree, proudly following Malcolm Lane, who was the first qualified Aboriginal ranger in South Australia. Ricky completed his degree about five years later. Ken and I have stayed connected over the years. Ken was always one of the blokes that you just look at and you can't help but laugh. His antics and his sayings still ring clear in my memory. They sometimes even haunt me at night. "Nah, only joking, ya nugget."

I found university to be a completely positive experience. It provided me with an endless supply of career choices and has set me up for life. I have had so many job opportunities since graduating that my only advice to anyone who is considering study at uni is, "Give it a go!" University was the stepping-stone I needed between the years of being a teenager and moving into adulthood. It taught me much more than academic knowledge. I look back and realise during those years I learnt about life, living, who I was and what I wanted to be. None of these were things I could have learnt anywhere else, and it wasn't stuff that I could have read from a textbook either. It was just something I had to experience for myself and, yes, sometimes I did make mistakes. However, the most important part of the process was that I learnt from those mistakes. (I must admit, sometimes I didn't learn, though — but don't tell anyone!)

I got my first proper part-time job while I was still studying at university. I undertook a traineeship with Elizabeth TAFE in Aboriginal education. I was a trainee lecturer in Introductory Vocation Education while I continued my own full-time studies. A couple of afternoons a week, I would go along to the local TAFE and work alongside the other Aboriginal education lecturers. I was fortunate that they also provided me with the opportunity to do formal training in the New Entry Lecturers Methods Introductory Course (NELMIC), which really gave me an insight into lecturing and working with adults. It was in this position that I had my first painful cultural learning experience with one of the Aboriginal students. This experience forced me to look at my own identity, and I began to wonder and question whether I would ever fit into this "black" world, while knowing that I also didn't belong completely in the whitefulla's world either. I was completely torn.

I distinctly remember an afternoon when I was walking around the class while the students were doing work I had set. One of the mature-aged Aboriginal men looked up at me and said in an offhanded manner, "Ya don't sound like a Nunga, and ya don't act like a Nunga!" I must admit, I can't remember what I said or whether I even responded to that statement. What I do remember was that it was like a slap in the face to me. I went home that night, absolutely boiling with rage. Rage at him, rage at myself, rage at my birth mother, rage at my adoptive family, rage at the government and rage at society, both black and white!

This comment forced me to realise that, yes, I was different, and yes, I would never fit into the mould of how most black or whitefullas think an Aboriginal person should look and sound. And yes, I was, and always will be, a member of the Stolen Generations. I had to accept the fact that I can't change my past, and I'm not to blame for what happened to me. I am the product of a system that tried to breed Aboriginal people out. I am the product of the White Australia or Assimilation Policy.

In that moment, I realised that most non-Aboriginal people didn't accept me or think of me as a real Aboriginal person, but at the same time, the blackfullas didn't think I was black enough either. I couldn't win. I was in no man's land. Once again, I found myself not belonging anywhere.

Every time I go to the hairdressers, you can guarantee that they will ask me, "I hope you don't mind me asking, but what nationality are you?" When I proudly tell them, "I'm Aboriginal," they say, "Oh, but you don't look Aboriginal." They say it like it's a compliment, and that I'm one of the lucky ones who could get away with being mistaken for Indian, Sri Lankan or some other ethnic community. I hated it, and hated that I didn't have the right words to shut them all up. These recurrent comments came from both black and white people and constantly reminded me I was trapped between two worlds. The most painful of them all was a saying that I've heard from other blackfullas and that is, "Ya nothing but a coconut." When I first heard that comment, I had no idea what it meant but didn't take long to work it out: you're black on the outside, but white on the inside, just like a coconut.

Constantly encountering what I've now come to recognise as "racist" comments left me feeling as though I didn't belong anywhere. I just didn't fit in either world. Even though, in my heart, I felt Aboriginal, I continually felt as though I needed to justify myself and my life in both the black and white worlds that I felt trapped between. At this point in an adopted Aboriginal person's life, you either head in one of two directions: you can get stronger and accept the predicament you find yourself in, or you can give in and consider yourself a victim of white Australian policies and give up. As for me, I just got angrier and thought to myself, "Nah, fuck it! I am Aboriginal, and I don't care what you think makes me Aboriginal. I have always been proud to identify as Aboriginal, and just because I don't fit your stereotype of what you think a black woman looks or sounds like, I'm not gonna change my appearance, the way I talk, my dreams, my goals, or my lifestyle, just to satisfy you for a moment in time."

Unfortunately, many Stolen Generations mob do crumble under the pressure of society. Always trying to conform to society's stereotypical depiction of what it is to be a "real" Aboriginal person. Most Stolen Generations mob continually seek ways to gain acceptance and a sense of belonging that will satisfy both their black roots and their white upbringing. Countless individuals have been torn between these two cultural identities as they struggle to find the balance of living happily in both worlds. Stolen Generations mob sometimes take on very self-destructive behaviours, just trying to find a way to fit in, be accepted or otherwise hide or numb their true feelings of pain and confusion. This often leads down a very slippery poor mental-health slope, and the only way back is through years of personal development and soul searching. What I have found is that you first need to make peace with your past, so you can live in the present, and then find that you can move freely into the future. As they say, "If it's to be, it's up to me!"

One comment that has brought me peace over the years is, "What you think of me is none of my business." It's really the advice that my adoptive mother should also have taken, but for years she kept running fearfully, worrying about what others were thinking of her. If you hang on to this saying you will find that you can become happy with who you are, what you look like, and how you choose to live your life. Yes, you still can search for the things you feel you missed while growing up. In my case without my Aboriginal birth family; but, most importantly, you will find that you don't have to be someone that you are not, just to make someone else happy. Be happy with who you are right now and continue to grow into the best person you can be. The best way you know how, and be the best version of your true self, whatever that may be.

I didn't know it at the time, but "the best way I knew how" to learn more about my Aboriginal culture was to find myself a mentor. For me, that was an Aboriginal Elder who gave me the cultural guidance and knowledge I was so hungry for, and desperately needed. Let me explain how I met Roger Thomas, who unbeknownst to him, was the mentor I needed at this very crucial time of my life.

After I graduated with my first degree — a Bachelor of Applied Science — I felt like the world was my oyster. I was a fully qualified Park Ranger who could work in national parks. The only problem was I didn't feel at all comfortable about getting out there and working in national parks. I decided to go on and do some more studies and undertook a Graduate Diploma in Education (Secondary Teaching). This took another year and a half of study, after which time I discovered, after working part-time at TAFE, that I was more interested in focussing on adult education than on high school kids. Once again, I didn't end up working in my qualification. Instead, I won a position as a project officer in the Aboriginal Education Program with TAFE.

How I came to win this position is an interesting story, and one that set me off in the right direction in life. It all started just before I left university when one of my lecturers, who happened to be American, taught me an unbelievably valuable lesson. He told me about a very articulate Aboriginal man whom he'd recently met. This man was the manager of an Aboriginal Education Program at TAFE in Adelaide. My lecturer suggested that I make an appointment to meet with him and let him know I'd recently graduated and was looking for work. The lecturer made it quite clear that I was to "speak directly to the manager and don't leave a message with the reception staff."

On his advice, I did exactly that! I'd ring daily, only to be told the manager was busy, but asked, "Would I like to leave a message?" Each time, I would kindly refuse to leave a message, then disappointedly hang up the phone, but vow to myself that I would try again the next day. I repeated this procedure until, finally, I managed to speak personally with the manager. Excitedly, with my heart in my mouth, I explained I'd recently graduated from university and that I wanted to make an appointment to meet with him to discuss my future job options. Amazingly, he agreed to meet with me. It was only after putting the phone down that I thought to myself "What the hell am I going to do now? Who do I think I am, and what do I have to offer in the workforce?"

To cut a long story short, I must have made an impression, because after putting me through an emotionally torturous interview including an on-the-spot written essay, I was provided with an opportunity to work for the Aboriginal Education Program at TAFE with my future mentor, Roger Thomas. This project officer position was later advertised, and I won it in my own right. I spent approximately two years in this position, with Roger as my manager and mentor. So, thank you to Dad who taught me to be persistent, and my brother Fenwick who taught me to never give up. It quickly became clear that I had been guided to work in this space with Roger. It was as if Roger intuitively knew the gaps in my identity and helped to fill those gaps by passing on his cultural knowledge through his words and wisdom, and also by providing me with a range of opportunities to learn through firsthand experiences. In those few years, I travelled all over

Australia, meeting a range of other Aboriginal people. I sat in a creek bed in the Anangu Pitjantjatjara Yankunytjatjara (APY) Lands, listening to the local traditional Pitjantjatjara land title owners' land council meeting, and then would find myself sitting around a table in Parliament House in Canberra, hearing about policies that affected our people. It was an amazing, life-changing, culturally fast-tracking lived experience. I can't give enough thanks to Roger, who was a major contributor to opening my eyes, and my world, to my culture, my Aboriginality, and my birthright. It wasn't until much later in life that I realised that Roger had also been somewhat disconnected from his culture and so understood why I needed a mentor like him, who knew what I was going through.

Chapter 6
Out of Place

When Rusty and I decided that it would be a good idea if we got married, there wasn't really any big romantic proposal, it was more like a mutual agreement between the two of us. We had a nice formal engagement dinner party at home with our closest friends, which gave Rusty the opportunity to show off his newly developed cooking skills as an apprentice chef. Our guests were quite impressed.

We gave ourselves one year to plan the wedding. I was determined to have my fairy tale wedding. I started planning early to ensure that I had everything just as I had dreamed it. As expected, all my hard work paid off, and the wedding day turned out to be perfect. We had sixty guests, which was a combination of my adoptive family, Rusty's family, and our friends. The one thing that I look back on and ashamedly realise is that there wasn't one other Aboriginal person at my own wedding. Out of sixty people, I often wonder: how did this happen? Why, at twenty-four years old, did I not have any other Aboriginal family or friends that I could invite to my wedding? Where were all the other Aboriginal people in my life? Upon reflection, this made me feel deeply sad.

What I realised is that, at that point in my life, I felt as though I was not part of the Aboriginal community, and this made me feel very much alone. Even after all my concerted efforts to work within Aboriginal organisations, the Aboriginal community still did not accept me. On top of this, I still had not found all my birth family, which left me very isolated from my own culture and surrounded by white friends who were the only people who seemed to accept me just as I was.

I remember years later; I overheard what I thought was a terrible saying from another Aboriginal person. He described some other Aboriginal people as "Nothing but a nine to five black." He was describing Aboriginal people who only work in the Aboriginal community during office hours, but outside of those hours, live their lives like whitefullas and don't have any connection or engagement with their own Aboriginal community. I recognised that, at the time, he was also describing "me." Yes, with shame I admit that in the past, I was one of those people. However, it was not by a conscious choice or from lack of trying to fit in and belong. Often it is quite easy for a blackfulla who has grown up in their community with their families to forget that there is a whole other world of "Stolen Generations" people who are still searching for their own families and desperate to belong. Us Stolen Generations mob are just doing our best to find out who we are and trying our best and hardest to fit into the community that often don't understand or want us to return, because we are just too different. Unfortunately, sometimes our search for identity, in the beginning stages, is between nine and five.

Three months after we got married, Rusty and I planned to go to England for a six-month working holiday. This was the first time that Rusty had returned to his country of birth, and the first time I was to leave mine.

I found travelling quite a scary experience, but one that we ventured into together. We stayed with my adoptive mum's sister, Aunty Maureen, in Maidstone, Kent, for the first few weeks then we went and stayed with Rusty's maternal grandmother in Lindfield, West Sussex, for the rest of our time in England.

We weren't in England awfully long before I fell pregnant. We had planned to start a family, but didn't think that it would happen quite so quickly. It certainly did not take long for reality to hit home, as the morning sickness started four weeks into my pregnancy and lasted until I was four months pregnant. Before I got pregnant, I thought that morning sickness was just as it sounds: a bit of feeling queasy in the morning, and then you are right for the rest of the day. I don't think it could have been further from the truth. Unless you have been pregnant and experienced morning sickness, you will not relate to this. I suffered from nausea and vomiting morning, noon, and night. This "morning sickness" had me vomiting at any time of the day or night, whenever the sight or smell of something didn't agree with me, which was just about everything, apart from water.

Along with feeling extremely nauseated all the time, I was also extremely homesick. I just wanted to go home; I hated being on the other side of the world, and I just wanted my mum. Despite feeling extremely sorry for myself, Rusty's Nan, who'd had four children, had no sympathy whatsoever and would simply say to me, "You know it's not an illness, being pregnant," bless her. To be honest, the way I was feeling, I thought I had been cursed with an illness, it just happened to be called pregnancy and nothing that she said to me could convince me that this sick feeling would ever subside and was a gift from God.

I remember one incident quite vividly. Rusty and I had booked a weekend trip from London to Paris. We flew out from Heathrow Airport and arrived at Paris Airport. We were standing in line waiting for our luggage and I could no longer fight the feeling to vomit. I knew I had to find a toilet and find it fast! I raced off at a fast pace in search of a toilet. Unfortunately for me, I couldn't speak French, and Rusty could string only a dozen words together.

As we were running flat out through the airport corridors, with Rusty racing ahead of me, I just knew that I wasn't going to make it to the toilets in time. Frantically, I looked for at least a rubbish bin to be sick in, but to my horror there were none whatsoever in the airport, which I later discovered was due to the risk of bomb threats. The next best thing was a shallow cigarette butt ashtray. Since I don't smoke and can't tolerate it, this only made my urge to vomit worse. Rusty was five metres ahead of me, and I tried to scream to him that it's too late: I was going to be sick, all the time trying to hold back the vomit with my hand and spreading my fingers over my mouth. If you've got the visual thing happening, you will know that it was not a pretty sight when the volcano erupted. It went through my fingers, on the floor and then splashed into the ashtray. It is only a guess, but it's quite possible that this is where the idea of garden fountains came from. I have never been so embarrassed in my whole life. That ashtray may as well have had a bomb in it, because after that the place cleared out like you wouldn't believe, everyone just scattered. It was the grossest thing I have ever done.

It sure was an adventure, and I've obviously lived to tell the tale; I must admit that we really did have a nice time in Paris, and I can laugh about it now. For any of you who are currently going through this stage of pregnancy, I can certainly sympathise with you, and can only reassure you that, thankfully, it does subside, and a beautiful baby is born at the end of it all.

While we were in England, we had the opportunity to experience the most wonderful things, and to this day I can hardly believe that it was a dream come true, and that I could tick off a goal from my bucket list. We went to English Heritage-listed properties that were full of history. All of these properties had some form of a big old castle built on them. They are just simply amazing to walk through, apart from feeling the eerie vibes — in other words ghosts — or, in South Australia, a commonly used Aboriginal word is "mamu", which is a Pitjantjatjatjara Western Desert word. I sure did feel like it was somewhat of a "guided" tour, if you know what I mean. We went to a medieval castle in Dover, which was built in the eleventh century — that's the 1200's. We also visited Leeds Castle in Kent, which was known as "the loveliest castle in the world." The original manor was built in 857 AD and was owned by a Saxon royal family. Over the years it has been home to six medieval queens and so it was also known as the "Castle of Queens." We went to Lewes Castle and Museum in East Sussex. It was one of the first castles built in England, it was a medieval Norman castle, built after the Battle of Hastings, between 1067 and 1070. It even had a moat. Nearby was Battle Abbey which was built as a memorial to the dead from the battle of Abbey. It was a very strange feeling, standing on the site of the Battle of Hastings, which occurred in 1066, and there I was, 926 years later, standing on the fields where between 6000-10000 soldiers were injured or killed. Such brutality and barbaric hatred over a struggle for the throne seemed so senseless. These atrocities seemed like such a foreign concept to me at such a young age, yet, back in Australia, there had been a genocide of my own people that I was totally unaware of. My schools had completely whitewashed and excluded the real black history of our country. It wasn't until I became an adult that I learnt about the true black history of this country.

Back to England, we also went to Canterbury Cathedral, which is one of the oldest and most historic Christian structures in England. It was founded in 597, and King Henry IV is buried at Canterbury Cathedral. Very strange. We went to Hampton Court Palace and Gardens, which in 1530's was a palace, a hotel, a theatre, and a big leisure complex. Lavish banquets, extravagant court life, and amazingly expensive art were once part of life there. We also visited the Archbishop's Palace, which was the official residence of the Roman Catholic Archbishop of Port of Spain. It was much more modern, having been built in 1969. We also saw Hever Castle, in Kent. It was built in the thirteenth century, was another medieval castle, and was the childhood home of Anne Boleyn, who later became Queen of England for 1,000 days. We finally visited Dartmouth Castle, which was built in 1388 and served as an artillery protecting Dartmouth Harbour in Devon.

We also visited general places of interest in London by travelling on one of those famous big old red open-top double-decker buses, which I used to see on old English TV shows that my parents used to watch when I was young. We saw Buckingham Palace, Piccadilly Circus, Trafalgar Square, Westminster Abbey, Big Ben, Hyde Park, Kensington Gardens and Kensington Palace, St Paul's Cathedral and we even passed over the Tower Bridge. The first thing that came to my mind during this was the old school song, "London Bridge is Falling Down." It was the weirdest feeling to be visiting those places that were part of my childhood memories. I instantly understood my mum's sayings, like, "this place is just like Piccadilly Circus," which indeed is a busy place. Even the old monopoly game took on a new light when I walked the streets that are the basis of the game.

We managed to see two theatre productions in London. One was "Miss Saigon", and the other — which was magnificent — was "The Phantom of the Opera" at Her

Majesty's Theatre. It's truly a phenomenal feeling to have dreamt about experiencing these things, and then actually going out and live your dreams. It was even better because I was so young and was able to thoroughly enjoy every moment of it.

It still puzzles me why people spend all their lives pouring money into their superannuation and saving for retirement, just so that they can start their once-in-a-lifetime adventures. Often, by this stage in their lives, their minds say yes, but their bodies say no. It really is a catch-22. It is just a decision that you must make in your life and just "do it!" This will mean giving up material things, so that you can enjoy lifetime experiences and memories, which are the only things we take to the grave.

In total, we were only out of Australia for four months, but that was long enough for me. I remember returning home and the first morning getting out of bed and going out the front of my mum's house. I couldn't help but appreciate and soak in the Australian environment around me. All my senses were truly alive. The colour of the sky, the colour of the trees, the smell of dew on the grass and eucalyptus from the gum trees was in the air, with the sun shining in the background and the familiar sound of all the Australian birds and their early morning calls. Before travelling overseas, I had taken all these things for granted. It truly opened my eyes to the extraordinary beauty that we have in this wonderful, unique country. It was also at this moment that I knew that, if I were to travel extensively again, it would be within my own country, rather than overseas. I felt like I'd just lived someone else's cultural dream and was pining to learn more about my own.

Chapter 7
Baby Coming Ready or Not

When we came back from England I jumped straight back into the workforce and worked right up until the time my firstborn baby, Jordan, was born. I had five weeks left until the due date and I went to the hospital for one of my last antenatal appointments. When I got into the cubicle, the midwife took my blood pressure, and it was quite high. She thought that it might have just been waiting-room nerves, so I had to wait a bit longer for another reading. Even after hours of waiting, my blood pressure still hadn't gone down, and I was told that I had pre-eclampsia, which is unusually high blood pressure during pregnancy, and that I wouldn't be going home today. Left untreated or undetected, pre-eclampsia can endanger the baby's health or my own, so I had to stay in hospital. I was in hospital for a couple of days when they decided to induce me so that the baby could be born early. It was quite funny because the day we were told that the baby would be induced was one year after our wedding day. That night, the nurses induced me, and I gave birth to a little baby boy at 9.45am the next morning. We named him "Jordan Rayne." I chose his middle name because I love the sound of rain on a tin roof, and I loved this little baby boy like I'd never loved anything or anyone in my entire life before. Finally, I had someone in this world who looked just like me and was a part of me. I couldn't have been any happier if I had tried.

Even though the nurses induced me to bring on my labour, I was happy with how everything had gone up until after the birth. It soon became clear that something was wrong when the hospital staff would not let Jordan and me go home after a week, yet I was confused as to why no one was really discussing their concerns with me. I know that I had experienced big fluctuation in emotion, and these are commonly known as baby blues. Women often experience these emotions a few days or weeks after the birth of a baby. However, in my case, after these first feelings, I started to lose all sense of time, and I just could not think properly. Everything was becoming very confusing. This is not a good state to be in after just having a baby. Even though I knew I was not right, I also knew I did not want to stay in hospital. I begged the hospital staff to release us, as I just wanted to get home and begin our new life with our newest family member.

Finally, they agreed, and we went home. Once we got home, my emotions and behaviour really started to change. I was an emotional wreck. Rusty, my family, and friends were obviously worried, but no one was able to pinpoint exactly what was wrong with me. I remember ringing my friends and talking to them on the phone. The only thing was that I was talking to them at a hundred miles per hour, flat out, describing every gory detail of the birth and hardly stopping to take a breath. This was one of the first signs that should have indicated to others that something was seriously wrong with my mental health. I also had an overwhelming sense of not being able to cope properly with just Rusty and me at home with a new baby. I demanded that we seek help from an Aboriginal family support service, thinking that this would make everything better and that then I would be all right. I was hardly sleeping, and I would have panic attacks at night, believing that if I did fall asleep, I was going to die. Rusty would rush me to the hospital for a thorough examination, only for them to give me all-clear and send me home. From memory, we went to the emergency department about three times over a period of three days.

The final straw was when I decided that I could not cope with bringing up this baby and that I would need help from my mum until I felt better and could manage things by myself. We headed off to Mum's, but once again, when night-time came, I could not sleep for fear of dying. I lay in bed next to Mum while she watched over me promising me that she would not let me die in my sleep. It was after this incident that, the next day, mum and Rusty encouraged me to go to the doctor. They wanted me to tell the doctor that they thought I was suffering from post-natal depression. With their encouragement, I finally made an appointment to see a doctor. I didn't even know what post-natal depression was.

I specifically remember sitting in the car while Rusty drove me to the doctor. Looking back, I could literally feel a surge of adrenalin pumping through my veins, which put me in a feeling of euphoria, like I was on a high and I could take on the world. When this feeling subsided, I would feel as though the tide had turned and the energy had washed away, leaving me flat and lifeless. It was in this pendulum of emotional states that I saw the doctor. Whilst sitting at her desk I explained all the events that had led me to this point. As I sat there, I was experiencing the peaks and troughs of adrenalin rushes. One minute I was laughing during the highs, and the next I was crying uncontrollably during the lows. The doctor took one look at me, prescribed anti-depressant tablets, and with that sent me home to continue to take care of our newborn baby. We ended up going back to Rusty's parents' house, as Rusty was busy helping his mum with the cooking for the upcoming Christmas Earth Fair.

As I had barely slept for four days, I was physically and emotionally exhausted; I was functioning purely on adrenaline. I took one of the prescribed anti-depressant tablets, had a little sleep, and woke up feeling as though the black cloud of doom I had been feeling had suddenly disappeared. I had a whole new lease on life and the world looked so much brighter and promising. I started to believe that I was suddenly well again; things would surely get better from here. I excitedly rang my adoptive dad in Bundaberg, Queensland, and promptly started to tell him all about my woes and how I had found a cure to my problems and, in fact a cure for all other post-natally depressed women. I then prophetically apologised for all the mistakes I had made with him in the past. You may remember that my dad had worked as a psychiatric nurse when he was younger. So, I know that hearing my voice over the phone would have been an immediate red flag for him.

After getting off the phone to Dad, Rusty's mum had cooked dinner, and I had built up an appetite. I sat down at the dinner table with Rusty, his mother, and his father. It was not long before I began to take over the entire conversation with more deep, thought-provoking theories about my condition, which is extremely unlike me. I was talking about how I was usually the dominant person in a relationship and everyone else was passive. After making the whole family feel unbearably uncomfortable with my uncontrollable talking, which did not make any sense whatsoever, I suddenly stood up at the dining room table and yelled, "I know what's wrong with me — I had schizophrenia before Jordan was born!" and with this announcement, I promptly ran barefoot out the front door and down the street.

With the adrenalin surging through my veins, I ran like a scared rabbit. I ran down the first alley I could find, trying hard to lose the trail of anyone who was chasing me. Where I was going, and what I was going to do, was beyond my thoughts, capabilities, or control. Normally, I am afraid of the dark and am an overly cautious person, but that night I felt like Superwoman. I could have taken on the entire world and more. "Bring it on", was what I said.

I ran to a complete stranger's house and banged on the screen door. An elderly woman opened the door, saw a deranged Aboriginal woman in front of her, and promptly slammed the door in my face. I ran to another stranger's house and banged on their door. This time a younger woman answered the door, but lucky for her she kept the screen door locked. "I'm sick, I need help. Please let me in so I can make a phone call," I begged her. There was no way she was gonna open that door, so I tried a new tactic. "Okay, can you take me to the hospital, or can you call my husband?" By this time, the messages in my brain were all getting completely jumbled and scrambled, and I could not make my brain function or think properly. I could not remember names or phone numbers or anything. I was a mess. Back in the day, there weren't mobile phones either. So, to make a call, I had to convince one of these neighbours to let me use their landline.

The adrenalin was still surging through my body, but now there was a good angel on one shoulder and a bad demon sitting on the other, working in tune with these adrenaline surges. The bad demon was possessing me during the highs, making me appear scary, threatening and demanding to the neighbours; "Open the fucking door. Can't you see I'm dying, and I need your help?" Meanwhile, the good angel was calming, soothing, and pleading. "Please just open the door, I promise I just need to use your phone that's all." These voices inside my head kept telling me to do conflicting things. The voices told me, "You need help, but when you get to the

hospital you will only have three hours before you will die."
The good angel would whisper words of reassurance. "It's
OK Joy everything's going to be OK." I knocked on another
house and found another woman who had two teenage
children who appear to be very scared of me. At the same
time, I could tell that they felt very compassionate towards me
and were begging their mum to help me. In the end, I ran
away from their house and ended up at one of Rusty's mum's
friend's houses.

I banged on their front door, and thank goodness they
were home. When she opened the door, I dropped like a sack
of heavy potatoes on the doorstep. The next thing I
remember, I was lying on the floor in her lounge, and she was
saying, "What's wrong Joy, are you okay?" Then suddenly, the
surge of adrenalin came pumping through my veins again. I
jumped up and screamed at the top of my lungs "I've won,
I've won, I've won, I'm a millionaire." I remember that I
started jumping up and down, holding hands, and jumping
around in circles with her as though we were playing ring-a-
ring-a-rosie. Then, once again, I dropped to the floor like a
sack of potatoes in exhaustion and passed out.

The next thing I remember is arriving in her car at the
Lyell McEwin Hospital emergency area. I remember a nurse
leading me into a small room, but upon realising that Rusty's
mum's friend was not allowed in, I started to panic. I was
screaming for her, "Don't leave me here. Help me. Come
back. They're gonna kill me. Help me. Don't you understand?
Help me. Please help me." By this stage, a hospital security
guard was standing there, blocking the door. He was a middle-
aged, balding, arrogant-looking man who was standing in my
way to freedom. Suddenly, the bad demon was back, sitting
on my shoulder, and I gave the security guard a mouthful of
foul language; I called him every name under the sun. "You

big fat fuckin white racist cunt, get the fuck outta my way, ya fuckin dog." No matter what I did or said, he still would not budge! Before I knew it, the good angel was back on the other shoulder, softly whispering in my ear, desperately trying to sweetly convince him that I was dying. "Please help me, I'm bleeding to death, I need your help, please." I could not work out why he did not care or understand about my imminent death. I stripped off all my clothes to try and prove to the security guard that there was blood all over them and that I was therefore dying and bleeding to death right before his eyes, which was false and not happening at all.

Eventually Rusty, Mum, and Uncle turned up, and they came into this tiny room to try and calm me down. By this stage now two security guards had me pinned down to the floor and I was kicking and fighting to save my life. In my mind I was dying and everyone else was out to kill me. I told them that I was bleeding to death and yet no one would listen to me. Everyone was down on the floor with me, trying to soothe me and calm me down. "Joy, it's gonna be okay. Just calm down." Yet the surges of adrenalin were still passing through my body. When the adrenalin was running through my veins, I was invincible, and I would fight and swear like you could not imagine. The ebb and flow of this chemical imbalance and fluctuation was completely draining. I was completely exhausted, but in my mind I knew I still had to fight for my life.

My prim and proper mother did not even know that I knew such filthy language. She placed her hand over my mouth trying to stop me from swearing. With my arms pinned down by everyone, she left me no alternative but to bite her hand. It was not just a little bite either, and it achieved the result I wanted. The nursing staff had to take mum out of the room to get her hand seen to. I can laugh now, but at the time it was the most terrifying experience I had ever had in my whole life. After this, I remember saying to Rusty, "Come here, I wanna tell you something. Come here, please." For some funny reason, he would not have a bar of it, he wanted to keep his ears, spoil sport!

Eventually, after what seemed like an eternity to me, a doctor came in wielding a huge syringe. Being in the mental state I was in, my first thought was that this needle was going to be the lethal injection that would kill me. If you think I fought them holding me down before, imagine how hard I kicked and screamed this time. With strength beyond human explanation, I was lifting the two security guards, Rusty, and Uncle off the floor. "Get away from me you fuckin killers. Get the fuck away." In my mind I had to do this because I was fighting for my life. Finally, the drugs took effect, and the next thing I remember is the ambulance officers strapping me down like a mad woman onto a hospital gurney and wheeling me into the back of an ambulance. After all the screaming, I was so thirsty, but they would not even give me a drink. Perhaps they had heard about Mum's earlier incident with her hand.

Dropping in and out of consciousness, the next thing I remember was the mental health hospital staff releasing me, like a wild animal, into a padded pink cell, which only had a foam, gym-like mattress on the floor. The hospital staff slammed the big door shut behind me with a huge echoing thud. Still naked, and thinking that I was about to die because of the injection the doctor had given me, I began to run in endless circles around the small room, chanting to myself, "Jordan and Rusty, Jordan and Rusty, Jordan and Rusty, Jordan and Rusty." I distinctly remember doing this, as I knew it was the only thing that would keep me alive through this horrendous experience.

I do not exactly remember waking up in the padded cell;
I just remember being told by one of the grumpy female
mental health nurses it was time to get up and have a bath. I
had no idea where I was, but that was the beauty of it all — I
did not have to think for myself. Everyone else was doing all
the worrying for me. It turned out that the ambulance staff
had transported me to a mental health institution called
Glenside. I remember walking through one mainstream area
of Glenside and seeing a huge black chalkboard which had an
enormous sketch of a lizard on it. I do not know if it was a
coincidence or not, as I seemed to be experiencing non-stop
coincidences during this time, but two months prior to this, I
had my tea leaves read, and this lizard looked exactly like a
magnified drawing of the figure from the tea-leaf reading. I
have been told by my sister Beverley that my totem is a lizard,
so I wondered whether this was of cultural significance. This
drawing silently comforted me in such a frightening and
unfamiliar place.

Chapter 8
No Shame

The experience just described was a postpartum psychotic episode. Postpartum psychosis, now referred to as puerperal psychosis is a psychiatric condition. It is a serious, but fortunately rare, perinatal mental health condition and only happens to about 2.6 people out of every 1,000 births. The first known case of this condition was described by Hippocrates in 400 BC. He documented a patient experiencing confusion, delusions and insomnia within six days of giving birth to twins. It is a mental health condition that severely affects some women after having a baby, and they can become quite psychotic after giving birth, but, with the proper care it is possible for the woman to recover completely, and quite quickly, from being "very mad." I was that woman. I lost touch with reality; I was seeing and hearing things that weren't there and I thought that many things were highly coincidental, my brain was completely jumbled, and I couldn't think clearly. I was also feeling completely paranoid.

You may be familiar with the baby-blues, or even post-natal depression, but few people are familiar with puerperal psychosis, which is the most severe of these conditions. The baby blues are a mild disorder and affect up to eighty percent of new mothers; post-natal depression can vary in severity and in the length of time that it persists. It affects between ten and forty percent of new mothers. The chances of puerperal psychosis occurring in an individual are relatively low. Back in 1996, when this occurred, I thought that I just must have been one of the unlucky ones and fate had just chosen me to go through this experience. What I have since come to understand is that you are more at risk of experiencing this condition if you already have a diagnosis of bipolar disorder or schizophrenia, and/or have a family history of mental health illness. Not knowing this when Jordan was born was very stressful and left me with many "Why me?" questions. However, over the years I realised that, of course, with my family history and Mum having schizophrenia, I was at high risk of experiencing this serious mental health illness.

Unbeknownst to me at the time, Rusty was an emotional mess. He had just witnessed me being driven by ambulance staff to a mental health hospital and to what he thought would be a future life of insanity, leaving him alone to bring up our newborn son. At the time I too thought that these mental health staff would hold me like a prisoner for a lifetime of insanity. I thought I would never get out and regain control of my life again. It was like I'd gone to prison and had all my rights removed.

I remember my intense frustration at this time because I was detained in a place where I felt I did not deserve to be, and once again I was somewhere I did not belong. When I reflect upon this time, I strongly believe that having Jordan triggered and released long buried and pent-up emotions relating to my own birth. Since having this experience, I've since realised that I had an undiagnosed complex post-traumatic stress disorder (CPTSD), and this exacerbated my already poor mental health condition. I may never be able to prove this connection, but I do know that having been through this traumatic experience gave me a true insider's perspective of perinatal mental health and how it impacts attachment with your baby, and how hard it is to repair those months, if not years, of damaged relationship with your newborn baby.

Two incidents are prominent in my memory about the brief time that I stayed in the North Glenn Annexe — Brentwood Ward — of Glenside Hospital. My mind was racing, and my brain was in overdrive. I had a multitude of thoughts going through my mind and I was very mentally and emotionally unwell. The only way that I knew how to get these thoughts out of my head was to do what I love, and that is write. I just needed a pen. I distinctly remember one of the mental health nurses sitting at the table with the other inpatients. All those patients looked about as off their faces on medication as I was. Yet they were sitting there with a lovely pencil case, happily writing and drawing away on paper at the table. Dragging my feet, I shuffled up to the table and asked in a slurred voice, "Can I please have a pen?" The carer looked at me and said, "No, you're not allowed a pen. You might stab someone with it!" I simply could not understand why all these other zombies were privileged with this basic right, and yet I was told I could not have a pen. After giving her a slurred mouthful of abuse, I returned to my room very disturbed.

Once in the room I settled down and started to plot and plan how I could get hold of a pen. Then I remembered that outside my room there was a whiteboard with marker pens on the ledge. As sneaky as a snake, I went outside the room and made sure that the wicked witch was not watching me, and then quickly stole the whiteboard marker and retreated to my room to start writing down the lists and ideas that were swimming around in my head. It was the relief that I needed. Despite the nurse's concerns, I did not use the pen as the weapon that she imagined; I used it in a much stronger way, through "the power of words." It was in this place that the birth of this book began.

The second incident I remember happened during lunchtime while I was in Glenside. The scene was like something out of the television show "Prisoner": We were all lined up waiting to get our plate of food, and then we had to choose a small table set for four at which to sit and eat our lunch. We were all walking like robots, with very disjointed movements, and no one really knew what anyone else was doing; we were all just going through the motions. When I was halfway through my meal, I realised that somehow, I had ended up at a small table with the only two other Aboriginal people. One was an elderly Aboriginal lady with wispy grey and black hair, who was cuddling a soft teddy bear. The other person on the table was a tall young Aboriginal man. None of us said anything to each other; it was just an instinct. It was as though the Ancestors drew us together, and even in our equally unhealthy states, we connected on a deep spiritual level. I do not know if either of them would even remember that precious moment, but for me it was much more than just sharing a table together. It was a symbol of the acceptance and unity that I had been seeking throughout my life, and one that will forever stay strong in my memory. In that moment, I felt connected to my Aboriginal identity and culture, and they were my family.

As my poor mental health was a result of having a baby, the hospital staff relocated me to a mother-and-baby unit called Helen Mayo House, within Glenside Mental Health Hospital. I did not get to go home with our son Jordan for another five weeks. During this time while they were trying to get my medication levels right, I experienced a roller coaster of emotions. After about three weeks, I no longer experienced high or lows. In fact, my mood levels were much more controlled, to the point that I just began to feel like my whole body was robotic and I was just a pincushion at the disposal of the medical world. My emotions were flat lining, not even a blip of life on the screen, one long emotionless drawn-out flat line. I didn't have any emotional highs, and I didn't have any emotional lows. I hardly knew what day of the week it was, never mind give a stuff about it.

This was an extremely tough time in which to bond with Jordan, as I was still having strange thoughts and would say things like, "I can't hold him, he's too heavy." It was during these tough times that I need to thank Rusty, but also our families and friends, for pulling me through and providing the love and affection that I was not well enough to give Jordan at the time.

While in the Helen Mayo Unit, one of my closest friends came to visit me and we decided that we would go to the local video store and hire a movie to help pass the visiting hours. Off we went to the video store to get a movie. We picked one, and I took it up to the counter, where I realised that I had to become a member to be able to borrow it. When the question of home address came up, I was not sure what to put, and, much to my surprise, the shop attendant had already decided that I must have been an escapee from Glenside, and he just discreetly said, "Are you from over there?" I said yes, but was wondering how this person, who had never met me before, knew where I was staying. As we walked out of the shop, I started to check my clothes and questioned my friend in a very paranoid manner, "How did he know where I was staying?" My girlfriend did not have the heart to tell me that I looked like a total wreck, and my eyes were so bloodshot that it appeared as though I had been on crack for a lifetime. Oh, to have friends!

During the five-week period that I spent at Glenside, I was continuously visited by well-meaning friends, and it really was quite a humbling experience to know that, when you are sick, you really do have friends who think about you and would really miss you if you were not around. I was trying extremely hard to get myself well, and I was searching for any method that would speed up the process so I could go home and get settled into the family life that I desperately wanted. However, that was not to be, and it took more lessons and mistakes before I just resigned myself to the fact that the only thing that was going to heal me was time.

What I really wanted was a spiritual healer, preferably a "Ngangkari" — a Traditional Aboriginal Healer — so Rusty searched around to find a spiritual healer who would see me. I am not sure how I knew that this was what I needed. It was as if I once again innately knew. It was part of who I was, and even though I'd never seen a Ngangkari at that point in my life, I knew it was what my spirit needed. Without any Aboriginal contacts, Rusty just went with one of his work mate's suggestions that his parents were spiritual healers. Desperate to try anything, the next weekend, Rusty checked with the staff at Helen Mayo to see if he could take Jordan and me out for the day, meanwhile refraining from telling them what he was really doing for me. They agreed, and we set off on a journey to goodness knows where, but I know it took a long time, and it was somewhere near Mannum, which is a small country town about an hour east of Adelaide. Anyway, we ended up at Rusty's mate's parents' house, and I cannot really remember too much about what happened, but I now realise that they were more like evangelists, and their definition of "spiritual healing" was quite different from my Aboriginal perspective and understanding of spiritual healing. I will never know whether what they did helped with my healing journey. I just wished I'd seen a Ngangkari, as I had wanted to.

Despite all the surrounding stress, Rusty still managed to go and work as a chef, and at the end of his exhausting days he would come back to Helen Mayo and care for Jordan and me.

I continued to insist that we tried to keep things as normal as possible, in the attempt to convince everyone else — me included — that everything was well and that I was returning to normal. To my disappointment, once again my attempts were sabotaged by the intense anxiety attacks that I would experience during outings I had arranged to attend.

Prior to having Jordan, Rusty and I would go to a movie once a month with a group of friends organised through one of our friend's work social clubs. I decided that I was feeling okay and since Rusty was at work, my friends arranged to pick me up and take me to see this latest released movie called "Jack" which starred Robin Williams. The nursing staff at Helen Mayo looked after Jordan for the few hours that I was gone. Just before they picked me up, I had changed Jordan's nappy, so when they picked me up I was convinced that my hands stunk of baby poo, although I had washed them thoroughly. After convincing me that they could not smell anything and that everything was fine, off we went.

Once the movie started, I began to feel jittery and had an intense urge to wriggle, then a dark cloud of claustrophobia came over me, and I just wanted to escape. This movie seemed intensely long, and when it finally finished, I just started to bawl my eyes out, crying uncontrollably and I desperately wanted to retreat to the safe haven of the Helen Mayo Unit.

Incidents like these continued to occur, and with each new panic attack, to my amazement, I would manage to conjure up another overwhelmingly convincing story as to why I could not be around crowds, travel in the car for lengthy periods, or stay at people's homes and talk for hours as we had previously been used to doing.

I vividly remember one incident leading up to the Christmas period when we were shopping at the local Big W store and, suddenly, a sweeping blanket of emotional pressure fell onto my chest and engulfed me like a tight rubber band. I could hardly breathe, and I just had to get out of the crowds. I believed I had diarrhoea, and I convinced Rusty that if he didn't get me out of there in two seconds flat, then they would surely be calling, "Mop and bucket to the toy aisle, please."

In a panic of his own, at the thought of this eventuality, Rusty convinced a store attendant that I desperately needed to go to the toilet. The next thing I knew, I was out the back in the staff-only toilets. Unsurprisingly, there was no diarrhoea; it was simply a mechanism for me to hot tail it out of an emotionally distressing situation. It gave me the refuge I needed in that moment. Looking back, I am amazed at how our minds work and what happens when our brain wiring gets crossed and the messages get muddled. Technology may be advanced today, but I can guarantee that no computer in the universe can compete with the human mind.

I liken my recovery from the postpartum psychotic episode to healing from a bruise. When you bump yourself and get a nice big bruise, and it really hurts at the time, and no matter what you do, it is inevitable that it is going to come up a real shiner. Then it goes from a red to a deep bluey-black colour and it is tender and too sore even to touch. After a while, it starts to change colours and turns yellow, and it no longer hurts to touch. In fact, it is so itchy it must be scratched, and you start to scratch around it until the entire bruised colour is flushed away and fresh blood and skin cells replace it. After a while, no one would ever have known that you had had a bruise unless you told them.

Metaphorically speaking, my postpartum psychotic episode was the biggest bruise I had ever had in my life. At the time it hurt like hell, and I did not want anyone to touch it. I was obviously hurting on the inside, and I was not a pretty sight to look at, as I'd lost all sense of self-pride and just couldn't be bothered trying to make myself look nice or pretty. Over time I gradually started to get better. It did not hurt so much on the inside, and I became more open to being loved again. Then, suddenly, I knew that my bruise was beginning to heal and I wanted to help it heal too. I started to try harder every day and made a big effort to achieve the trivial things in life, like making a cup of tea, washing my hair, tying my shoelaces. It was these small feats that indicated that I was on the mend.

The main indicator of my gradual healing was the fact that I once again became aware of time. Before this, I had forgotten that clocks even existed and that everyone marched to the beat of a tick-tock clock. I started to notice when the staff shifts changed, and I would eagerly await Rusty's return from work. I started to remember what day of the week it was and how far away the weekend was. I would remember what my favourite TV shows were, and was able to sit down, concentrate, watch them, and understand what was going on. I would sit and watch new mothers and their babies come into the unit, and have conversations with them and think to myself, "Gee, they are really sick, and they need help." I could see how strange the things they were saying about themselves and their babies sounded.

After about two earlier attempts at going home for one-day visits, the time came when I could go home and stay home with our baby Jordan. I knew that there was still an exceptionally long road ahead of me, and I relied on my family and friends for that extra support during this time of healing. It really was a slow recovery to full health and wellbeing, but I accepted the challenge, and it took a good year before I began to feel as though I was getting back to my old self.

For about ten years after Jordan's birth, I resented this episode in my life. However, after having had two more children, I can look back and deeply appreciate all the lessons that this experience taught me. I now know that, without this challenging time; I would not be as appreciative of the other positive and beautiful aspects of being a mum. Without having this experience, I know that I would have taken these things for granted. Without having had this harrowing experience, I wouldn't have ever wanted to learn more about puerperal psychosis, and I wouldn't have gone on to understand attachment theory and become a Circle of Security Facilitator or a specialist in Perinatal Infant Mental Health. So it is with pride that I can now look back and realise that I had to go through this, so that I can help others learn about it and, hopefully, avoid it.

Now instead of asking, "Why me?" I can think, "Why not?"

After Jordan was born, I was not in any state to work; I was barely able to take care of myself, let alone a newborn baby. Somehow, I coped, and I stayed home raising Jordan for the first eight months of his life. I was what is known as a "good enough" parent. It wasn't great, but it wasn't that bad either, it was good enough.

Before I had Jordan, I bumped into an old school friend who already had a six-month-old baby. While I was sick in the hospital, this girlfriend had kindly offered to clean my house. Not surprisingly, when I came home from the hospital, I found myself latching onto her through the first six months of my recovery. Every morning, Jordan and I would end up at her little flat and we would just spend the entire day with her and her baby. When I look back now, I cannot believe how patient she must have been with Jordan and me. I was drugged up to the eyeballs, and hardly made any sense, but she never once turned me away. For this, I thank her with all my heart! God rest her soul.

By the time Jordan was eight months old I was feeling better, and things were starting to make sense and feel a bit normal once again. I began to take notice of the things that were happening around me, and life slowly started to have meaning, and day by day I was getting emotionally and mentally stronger. One day, unexpectedly, I decided that I wanted to become a "beauty therapist." Rusty was completely supportive of my whimsical desire and took me into Adelaide, where I enrolled mid-year into a full-time certificate of beauty therapy at the Heather Langton Academy of Beauty Therapy. I look back and can hardly believe that I did this. I had gone from fortnightly check-up visits at the northern mental health unit at Salisbury, where the staff told me that I could expect to stay on my antipsychotic mood-stabilising medication, lithium, for the rest of my life. Opting not to do this, I decided to start a fresh career path and life. It was the best self-medication I could have ever prescribed. I do not recommend or advise doing this without proper medical advice. While studying for my certificate in beauty therapy, there were about twenty other young women studying with me. I was the only Aboriginal student. Every day, all of us girls would pamper each other with massages, facials, manicures, or pedicures. I had a purpose to get up for, and I was doing something new, exciting, and glamorous every day. Slowly, through the year, my self-esteem and self-confidence grew again. I was gradually blossoming like a flower. I loved what I was doing and learning, and I excelled in my studies. I made two especially beautiful friends, Jaye-Leanne and Felicity with whom I still occasionally see, and we shared so much laughter and tears together that I will always remember them. I will always cherish the days I spent learning my new trade, and I know in my heart that it was what saved my life and brought back my sanity. For this I am forever grateful! During the days, Jordan would go to childcare, which was a blessing that helped me to repair my mental health. As the year went by, Jordan was growing and developing beautifully, and I was learning how to love him all over again.

When I finished my training as a beauty therapist, I worked for an Adelaide based natural skin care company and really liked that. This did not last long, as I wanted to set up my own beauty and waxing business at home. I did this and it was a year later that I won the job as a caseworker with the South Australia Link-Up Program.

Without realising it at the time, my taking on the South Australia Link-Up job was the start of a new chapter in my life. As the saying goes, "Life is like a book. Some chapters are sad, some are happy, and some are exciting, but if you never turn the page, you will never know what the next chapter has in store for you."

After working at South Australia Link-Up for a year, the metaphoric door that closed in my life was my marriage. By this stage, Rusty and I had been married for five years and had been together for seven years prior to that — twelve years in total. Jordan was 4 years old, and I had not had any urges to have any other children. My experience of Jordan's birth was still relatively fresh and painfully etched in my memory, and I was just starting to regain my confidence, freedom and sense of self and beginning to feel as though I was getting back to normal. I did want more children eventually, but just not now.

I was working full-time at South Australia Link-Up, and I was in my glory helping so many other adopted or Stolen Generations people find and reconnect with their birth families. I must admit that I found this job emotionally challenging but hugely rewarding because it was close to my heart. Yet the more I found myself becoming emotionally involved with the clients and their own journeys of finding out who they really were, the more my desire grew to find out who I was and connect with my own culture.

I honestly look back on those years during my separation and eventual divorce and question my own judgement. The only thing that I can put it down to is the common theme that has run through my life, which was the desire to find out who I really was. I now know that, at the time; I was still really confused about who I was. I was still searching and looking for answers to the plaguing question of "Who am I?" I know that it was my search for the answer to that question that led me to search in the wrong place. Without doubt, I was searching for the answers outside of myself, and all the time the answer was, and always has been, within me.

I have analysed those years, months, and days that led to the eventual breakdown of my twelve-year relationship with Rusty, and I cannot pinpoint a moment in the relationship when I thought, "I don't love you." I just felt as though I gradually grew out of love with him. I loved him, but I was not in love with him. We were comfortable being comfortable. We both still tried to be a strong couple, and we would still do special stuff for each other, and I know that our friends thought that we were the "perfect" couple.

I must admit that, yes, I knew what the consequences of my decision to leave Rusty would mean, and I did weigh it all up. Yet my desire to find my cultural identity continued to rule my life and drove me straight into the arms of another man — in fact, a strong black man. I know that this completely devastated Rusty and it was not something that either of us could have imagined would end our marriage. This was especially true after everything we had been through together and all the memories we had built up over the years. Yet amid the break-up, despite feeling deeply saddened by my loss, I also felt, at the same crazy time, as though I was about to gain so much.

I am not proud of my decision to leave, even though it was no more than a fling. Yet it felt so real, and it felt right. I was so confused, yet for once in my life I felt like this "black" man really understood me and accepted me for who I was. I thought that I was finally complete. I finally felt like a real "black woman". This fling resulted in the complete breakdown of my marriage. At the time, I did not care who I hurt because I was "in love".

My search for freedom to express who I really was finished before it started, and I found myself a single woman within weeks of when my whirlwind fling began. Once again, I experienced a huge sense of rejection and abandonment. I had given up everything I knew and everything with which I was familiar and identified with. I was once again alone in this world. I could hardly bear my own presence. I hated being single, I hated my quiet house, I hated feeling alone, and I hated myself. What I didn't realise in that moment was that where hate is, love is not, particularly self-love.

I thought I needed someone else to make me feel complete. I began questioning again: Who am I? I discovered that I still really did not know the answer to that question. Instead of feeling empowered by my freedom to be me, I wanted to find another mate to fill the emptiness and rejection that I was feeling inside. My search for my identity started all over again and I thought that this time I would be able to find it at the bottom of a bottle, or through another black man who would really understand and accept me. I felt like I had completely changed overnight. If ever I didn't know who I was, it was in this exact moment.

For the first time since being a teenager, I ventured into a pub and began going to nightclubs. I drank alcohol and danced all night till the early hours of the morning. I loved the feeling of being drunk because I did not have to think about my problems, because they all magically disappeared. I could be whoever the hell I wanted to be, and everyone accepted me. I could dance with abandonment and not have a worry in the world. The only problem was that, when I woke up in the morning with a screaming headache and crook guts, I realised that I was still the same lost soul I had been the day before I started drinking and partying. This cycle of my life was short-lived, and it was not as bad as it sounds, but for me, it was an indication of the hate that I felt towards myself. This was my attempt at self-destructing. I wanted to destroy everything that I had previously worked so hard to achieve. I wanted to hurt myself and punish myself for the pain that I had caused others. I wanted to be numb. I didn't want to feel anything. I wanted to run away but had nowhere to run to. What made it worse was that I realised that despite this pain, I still did not know who I was.

At my lowest point, I thought it best to add a bit more drama into my already turbulent life. This time, in the form of a "toxic" relationship that just seemed like a complete waste of my time. This relationship stripped me of the last few layers of my barely repaired self-esteem. I thought that by being with another black man I would once again find my identity as an Aboriginal woman. I must admit that, over the next couple of years I did find out some more things about "being black", but not much of it was positive or a true reflection of my Aboriginal culture.

I quickly discovered how controlling an insecure person can be, and how they can quickly wear you down to a point where you start to question your own thoughts and beliefs. Controlling people like this are the ones with poor self-esteem, they only have one way of making themselves feel better: usually by making you feel worse. I started to believe that I was wrong, that I was to blame, and that I was guilty of everything. This toxic power and control freak was constantly questioning my faithfulness, "Why are you looking at him?" He would accuse me of wanting every man I saw. I was questioned about why every man was looking at me. He'd say, "I bet you're fucking him too. I know everyone wants to fuck you," and, according to him, I was also fucking my adoptive brother. The list was endless, and the accusations were relentless. I quickly became worn down and was walking around on eggshells trying to keep the peace. I did not feel safe in my own home, and I never knew from one day to the next what to expect.

Looking back, I can see that it was not a pleasant way to live, and I realise that I did not enjoy it. I also realised that, when I went searching for love, what I attracted was more hate. This person was clearly full of self-hatred and projected his toxic waste straight onto me. Strangely enough, I still stayed in that toxic environment for much longer than I should have. It was as if my self-esteem was so low that even I began to believe the lies that he was constantly spitting at me. I now know that over the years I have just made questionable choices, especially in the relationship department, but as I always say there is a reason for everything and if nothing else, I thought I had learnt what I do not want in a relationship. The lesson I learnt was: do not look outside yourself for love! You must learn to love yourself before you can love anyone else. When you learn to love yourself there is no need to search for love elsewhere, even if you are in a relationship. Whatever another person brings to the relationship is a bonus.

After my toxic relationship, my thoughts turned back to my unresolved grief and guilt about the breakdown of my marriage, and the hurt and pain that my actions and choices had caused surrounding the fling. I knew to overcome this feeling of guilt I had to take complete responsibility for my own actions and accept my past for what it was. The one thing that I have learnt is that no one can make you do something you do not want to do. I have also learnt that no one can make you change what you do not want to change. The only person that has control of your life and can change your life is you!

During the toxic relationship, I was an emotional wreck. I put up a front for everyone and never let the world know that on the inside, I was dying and full of guilt and shame. My self-esteem was at its lowest and I did not feel beautiful, smart, strong, proud, or loved. I now know that the only person that can provide you with those things is you. However, at the time I felt as though I needed to hear and feel those things externally, from outside of myself, from someone else and I did not believe in my own inner beauty, so I continuously sought compliments, approval, and love from outside myself. Before I knew it, I found myself back in the same predicament and had restarted my fling, which had now become an affair.

I hate the word affair because it sounds so dirty and sinful. We were having not only a physical connection, but also an emotional relationship and it was not as sordid and immoral as everyone made it out to be. Instead of feeling ashamed of this "dark secret" and hoping that one day it would magically disappear from my lifetime experience list, I needed to bring it out into the light and let the world know what I learnt from this experience.

Unless you have had an affair, then you cannot judge or understand the feelings that drive it. My affair was exciting; it made me feel beautiful, special, connected, wanted, needed, loved and happy. It made me feel like my life was still worth living. It made me feel like a beautiful strong Aboriginal woman. These were all the things that I was missing at the time, and these were the things I hadn't yet learnt to give to myself ~ self-love.

I want to make it clear at this point that, much to most people's surprise, affairs are not just about sex. Yes, sex was involved, but it was more about meeting each other's emotional rather than sexual needs. That is just from my perspective as a woman. I have also worked out that most men think sex equals love. This is how they get their emotional needs met. It is simple, but we do tend to complicate it.

Chapter 9
Carrying Them Through the Flames

Now the saying goes, "When you play with fire, someone gets burnt," it also hurts, leaving a scar and a tarnished reputation that always reminds you of a sordid past. During my toxic relationship, plus my affair, I managed to get pregnant. More drama was the exact opposite of what I needed in that moment! Sometimes, instead of finding a healthy way to get out of a destructive, dysfunctional relationship, when we are not strong enough to make better choices for ourselves, the Universe and our Ancestors step in to supply a solution. I can guarantee that, at the time, it sure did not feel like a solution; it felt like my world had once again crashed around me. I was so confused; I knew that I did not honestly know the paternity of this baby, and I knew that I did not want to bring another child into this world, or into the life that I was leading. Something had to change. I knew that based on my own values having a termination was not an option. So, I just took each day as it came, one day at a time. I finally decided that it had been seven years since I had had Jordan, that the time was now right, and that I would have this baby and just be a single mum. I had faith that the future would take care of itself. I know that this baby chose me and forced his own perfect way into this world, whether I was ready or not.

The next thing that happened was not in my master life plan and I am not even certain how it came about. I knew that

I craved stability in my life, and that I did not want to bring up a baby alone. I knew after having such an ordeal with my first son Jordan, who was now living in a shared care arrangement between his father and me, that I would struggle as a single parent.

Once again, my pattern of abandonment kicked in, out of fear of being alone. I found myself jumping from one relationship to another, which meant that I made a choice to leave my past affair and get out of the other toxic relationship that I had been in. Straight into the arms of yet another black man. This is how I came to be with my next partner, whom I have come to describe as the Puppeteer. He was a psychological manipulator who took pleasure in mentally harassing me and distorting my reality for his own amusement.

The Puppeteer and I vaguely knew of each other in high school, yet we never really got to talk because he was too shy and thought that I was a snob. The Puppeteer appeared to be a very kind-hearted, gentle, and quiet person. He was Aboriginal and seemed extremely comfortable in his own identity. He grew up in Adelaide with his mum and his dad who had separated when he was young. Both of his parents are proud Aboriginal people. I met the Puppeteer again not long after I had split up with Rusty — my ex-husband — but even after giving the Puppeteer my number in the nightclub, he never actually called me. I thought nothing of it, and it was not until about two years later that our paths crossed again. It is quite strange how life pans out, but this time I thought it was meant to be.

My best friend at the time lived in a semi-detached house in the northern suburbs of Adelaide, and it just so happened that one day I turned up there, only to discover that the Puppeteer had moved in next door. At the time I was in the toxic relationship, and I did not think that I was looking for love. Sometimes you do not consciously look for love, and it just comes searching for you. I did not plan to start a new relationship, but the Universe our Ancestors had other plans. The Puppeteer had recently separated from a long-term relationship and had a similar wounded soul. This was a common bond that we had. I felt like I could instantly relate to the pain that he was going through. I thought I could rescue him, which I have since discovered I tend to love doing. I have since discovered this common bond is known as trauma bonding. It involves a victim and a perpetrator traumatically bonding with each other. The victim is often unable to leave the relationship or is only able to do so with significant distress and difficulty. Even among those who do manage to leave, many go back to the toxic relationship because of the familiarity that the trauma provides. It sounds insane, but explains so much about domestic violence and the unfathomable reasons why so many people, usually women, including me, stay instead of leaving. Unfortunately, it took me sixteen years to break this toxic cycle and leave the relationship, in August 2020.

The Puppeteer was a hard worker, and it seemed that we had similar interests. Since finishing school, he travelled a lot, he had lived in both Mount Isa, Queensland and Alice Springs, Northern Territory. I loved travelling too, and the thought of getting on the open road again and exploring Australia with someone adventurous was a drawcard.

Without even trying, we developed a strong friendship that gradually shifted into something more serious. I dreamed of sharing my future with him and thought that he could provide me with a solid foundation from which my children and I could grow. I did not know how it would happen, but I believed that it would come true.

When the Puppeteer and I got together at the beginning of 2004, I was already three months pregnant with my second baby, who seemed determined to be born. At the time, I did not really think about the significance of what the Puppeteer had done, but I now look back and think about his decision and am grateful that he was there through that stage of my life.

However, I do not want to give the wrong impression, because the Puppeteer was not the type of guy that would mollycoddle you. He came from a life of hard knocks, and he really did not put up with too much of the emotional baggage that I brought into our relationship. It might be what is known as "tough love." Take it or leave it. It was this approach that helped me to hold my emotions together when my second son, Jay, was born.

Looking back to when Jordan was born, and the postpartum psychotic episode I experienced, it is understandable that I was not looking forward to a replay of that scenario with my second pregnancy. So, when I had my second baby, I went to the Adelaide Women's and Children's Hospital and made sure that I booked in with a psychiatrist early in the pregnancy. I wanted to make sure that I was prepared and did everything I could to avoid a recurrence of my earlier postpartum psychotic episode. Once again, I experienced pre-eclampsia (high blood pressure during pregnancy) and had to be admitted to hospital before my due date and was induced to bring the baby on early. The Puppeteer had already decided that he did not want to be there when my second baby was born, and I was fine with his decision. I remember asking my best friend, Rebbecca, at the time if she would come with me, which she did. Jay was safely born, and then it was just a waiting game to see what my emotions and hormones would do. I remember when he was born, and they handed him to me; it was love at first sight, and as soon as I saw him, I knew exactly who his father was. He had the blackest head full of hair and the sweetest little face. His little fingers curled around my finger, and I prayed to my Ancestors that he would never let go. I knew from that moment that everything was going to be fine. This time as a mum, I could just feel that things were going to be different and simply perfect.

For the first time, I was able to breastfeed. I was so proud of myself because it was something I had missed with Jordan. I decided to call him Jai, pronounced Jay, and his middle name was the same as mine, Lee. He was my little me. It wasn't until he became a teenager that he wanted to change the spelling of his name, to Jay, and his surname to reflect who he thought he was.

We didn't need to stay in hospital long, and Jay and I were home before we knew it. It didn't take long to get Jay into a lovely little routine and there was absolutely no sign of post-natal depression, let alone another psychotic episode. Yet, I cannot say that I was entirely with it, because I was drugged up to the eyeballs on preventative antipsychotic medication. Despite this, I do still remember these first few weeks and months much more clearly than I did when Jordan was born. I am forever grateful to have experienced a relatively normal pregnancy and birth. My most favourite times were the middle-of-the-night feeds. I still had my rocking chair that I'd had when Jordan was born. In the middle of the night, I'd get up, and it was just me and Jay rocking away. I'd lovingly look down at his beautiful little face and thank my Ancestors for the blessing of being a mother.

When Jay was twelve weeks old, we made a "spontaneous" decision to go to Darwin. It was a huge decision, and with every choice there's always consequences.

I never really told many people, but the night before we left, the home phone rang, and I picked it up and heard someone say, "Tell the Puppeteer (pseudo name) I know where he lives, and I'm gonna come there and slit his throat." Now, it probably sounds random, but the night before that phone call, the Puppeteer and his mates had been out drinking, and an all-in pub brawl broke out. This idiot, "the Puppeteer", went screaming his name at the top of his lungs, telling every bikey in the pub, who he was, and that no one fucks with him. It didn't take a rocket scientist long to track him down, putting not only his own life, but more importantly, my son's life and mine at risk.

So, by the next morning, we took off from Adelaide with Jay safely strapped into his baby seat in the back of the car and we headed north. At this stage, the Puppeteer had still been very wary of getting close to Jay, I suspect he was in fear of Jay's birth father re-entering the scene. The Puppeteer had hardly even held Jay, let alone bonded with him. This trip, however, changed everything. There was just the three of us.

Jordan, my eldest son, did not come to Darwin with us. By this stage, Jordan was living with his dad. Rusty and I thought it would be best that Jordan stayed in Adelaide in a stable environment. This was a difficult decision I had to make, and I know that Jordan, who was 8 years old, had no idea of what was really going on and felt a huge sense of abandonment, and I am truly sorry for this decision, I understand that it is one of those scars in life that we both now bear from choices that I was forced to make. Please forgive me, I'm sorry. Thank you. I love you more than you will ever know.

By the time we got to Darwin, we had covered much of this beautiful Australian country. The landscape was forever changing and breath-taking. The other changing element was the weather. It was February which is in the middle of an Australian summer. Thank goodness for air-conditioning, because it was so damn hot you could fry an egg on the bonnet of the car. It was a hot, sticky type of heat that made you feel like you had just stepped into a sauna. It was so humid and muggy that I could hardly breathe. I cannot say I was very fond of it. In fact, I hated it. Give me a cold, rainy day, snuggled up in bed under the warm covers, any time.

When we got to Darwin, we stayed for the first few weeks at my stepbrother's house. He and his wife had a granny flat that was just fantastic and suited us right down to the ground. We settled in quite nicely and Jay was just thriving. He was such a placid little baby; nothing really fazed him. After about three weeks we decided that it was time that we got our own space, and we found a little two-bedroom unit in Palmerston. It was perfect. I loved it. Jay had his own little bedroom, and we had ours. The Puppeteer managed to find a part-time job with homecare, and we had everything we needed.

I absolutely loved looking after Jay by myself during the day. It was the first opportunity I had had to prove to myself that I was a good mother, and that, yes, I could do it by myself. I just wanted to convince myself that I did not need anyone else to help me, and that I could do it just fine. I shocked myself and gradually my confidence in my parenting skills began to grow again. I know now that my attachment to Jay was strong. This is what I'd wanted so desperately with Jordan, but, due to my poor mental health, Jordan and I didn't quite achieve it together.

While we were in Darwin, I had lots of time to do the things that were of particular interest to me. I was studying part-time externally, finishing off my Masters in Social Science (Counselling). In between my assignments, I spent hours searching the internet looking for things of interest to read. I came across many articles that increased my interest in the healing principles, practices, and philosophies of Aboriginal and other cultures.

It was as though everything started to pull together and form a concept that I needed to develop and share. I really cannot explain it, other than I knew it was my destiny to explore this information further. I was becoming aware of knowledge that our Ancestors had known all along. I could see the holistic healing principles and the benefits of this wisdom, and knew that I had to somehow record it in a way that I could then share for the benefit of both Aboriginal and non-Aboriginal people. I now realise that this was the humble beginnings of my purpose in life, and it is what has driven me ever since.

I developed my life purpose statement which is: "To love, heal and educate as many people as I can." This is what drives me every day. It is what I get out of bed for, and it is what I go to bed thinking about at night. I just know that it is what I was put on this earth to do. I know that my purpose allows me to work with my strengths, and it also uses the challenges I have experienced in my life to help me reach others who have had similar experiences. I know it is the gift that I have been born with.

Now, I know that, yes, I also have three university degrees, and you might be thinking: "Of course you found your life purpose, you were given every chance." We all have a purpose in life, and it is just a matter of taking a close look at our lives, our history, our strengths, our weaknesses, and the things that interest us most. As soon as we take all those ingredients and blend them together, we end up with what's known as our life purpose, and life finally becomes meaningful. It's about finding out what your calling is and what speaks to your heart. What is it that you find yourself doing and realise you've lost track of time? What would you do even if you were not paid to do it? Answer these questions, and you will soon know what your purpose in life is too.

When we were in Darwin, I missed Jordan immensely, and after two months Mum and Jordan flew up from Adelaide for a fortnight's visit during the school holidays. I loved having Jordan with me again. It was also a special time for him to get reacquainted and bond with his little brother Jay. After Mum and Jordan went back to Adelaide, I knew that I could not stay in Darwin any longer. I missed Jordan too much and so I decided that I was going to return to Adelaide. Despite the Puppeteer wanting to stay and put down roots in Darwin, he followed my lead, and we drove back to Adelaide together.

On our way back we decided to travel through Queensland, and stopped off in Bundaberg to see my adoptive dad. I know that the Puppeteer really enjoyed meeting him and it was good for Dad too, as he could finally accept that I had long ago divorced Rusty and was now with the Puppeteer.

When we finally arrived back in Adelaide, we had to find somewhere to stay and get back into the rhythm of working life again. It was not long before we found another house to rent, and life started to settle down. By this stage, I had managed to have a year off with Jay, and that was just fantastic. That year really provided him with a well-balanced start in life and it has seen him thrive ever since.

I had not been back in my substantive position as an Academic Adviser at the University of South Australia for long when I realised I was pregnant with my third child. Nine months later, my baby girl, Violet was born. I don't think that, before Violet was born, that I'd really fathomed the concept that she was a little girl. Having had two boys, Jordan and Jay, it felt natural that she was going to be a little boy too, so it really was strange to be using pronouns for a little girl. When she was born, I stared at her little angelic face and thought that my heart would explode. She was perfect. She looked like a perfect little porcelain doll. Her beautiful little lips and her cute little nose. Just like her brothers she also had a head full of hair. I knew that I was the luckiest mum in the world, to have created such a beautiful little girl and to have been blessed with three beautiful children.

Before Violet was born, the Puppeteer and I did not want to know the sex of the baby. I was happy about that because I reckon that, after all that pushing during labour, you sure would want a welcome surprise at the end. Thankfully, this time the Puppeteer did decide that he would come in for the birth. However, it was not until after it was all over that I discovered that the Puppeteer really doesn't have the stomach for anything quite as confronting as labour. I did wonder why he was sitting in the corner of the labour room, looking very anxious and pale, rocking like a baby while chewing his fingernails. Over the years, it wasn't unusual to see the Puppeteer lying flat out on the cold tiles on the floor, trying to get his anxiety and phobias under control. It always made me laugh, which is probably a bit cruel on my part, but, admittedly I didn't understand trauma responses back then like I do now.

Once baby Violet and I got home, all plans were in place in case of a recurrence of a postpartum episode; thankfully, all was well this time too. Violet was a colicky baby, and every night at six o'clock on the dot she would start crying in pain. Nothing settled her, and both the Puppeteer and I would walk around the house rocking her and laying her on our stomachs, trying anything to settle her. I would cook dinner with her strapped to my stomach in a baby sling, just for a few minutes of peace and quiet. This went on for the first six weeks of her life. It sure was a challenge and I am glad those baby days are over. In desperation, I went to a health food store, and they gave me acidophilus tablets. I cannot guarantee one hundred per cent that they worked, but I do think that, by taking these friendly probiotic bacteria for my stomach and intestines, I helped Violet via my breast milk, and, as the months went on, she seemed to settle into family life. Or, who knows, perhaps I'm the one that finally settled, and she sensed that.

All my children have now well and truly completed high school, and are all working. Jordan has a car-detailing business; Jay works in scaffolding and has a love for playing AFL football like no other person I know; and Violet dreams of being a psychiatrist, but now she's happy to earn money working in the finance industry.

After Violet was born, life felt settled. Up to this point in our relationship, the Puppeteer and I had been like any average couple: we had travelled a bit, came back, settled down again, rented a house for a while, had Jay, and then, only twenty-two months later, had Violet. The Puppeteer had an older son, and he and Jordan would come and go as we worked around the various shared care arrangements. We decided to buy a house, and we also got a caravan to take away for our holidays. The Puppeteer did renovations to the shed and turned it into a rumpus room, and we just got into a little routine of what we did every day, week, month, and year, and before we knew it, nine years had flown by. When Jay and Violet were toddlers, life was good. Whenever we got the chance, we would hook up the caravan and head off on a little family holiday; sometimes we would head towards the beach or other times towards the river. We would go to the local annual Aboriginal Football and Netball carnival and go to family functions; smile, laugh, and have fun. The kids had birthdays, all of which we would happily celebrate together, and then wait for the next year to come around. The kids were growing at a rapid rate, and our wings were beginning to spread with the new freedom of their growth. Friends and family would come and go, and too many died before their time. We grieved together, and we healed together; we fought, and we made up. Up to this point, I trusted him one hundred per cent, and never doubted his faithfulness to our relationship or me.

It certainly did not seem to take long for five years to pass after Violet was born. I thought that things were travelling nicely when unexpectedly my world was once again turned upside down. I say unexpectedly, but in fact, upon looking back, there were dozens of signs, and I simply did not take notice of them. The end of 2011 and most of 2012 were full of drama and life lessons. I know that life can sometimes get hectic, but I did not think that I wanted or needed any more havoc. The powers that be thought differently and I suspect it was just my time to grow some more.

During the end of 2011, my mum was in the final stages of cancer, and this was a tough time. Mum had decided to start chemotherapy, but then decided, after two visits, that it just was not worth the pain and suffering that her body had to endure for the minimal extension of life that it vaguely promised to give her. Even though I was hoping for a miracle cure I knew deep down that this would not be the case. It was just a matter of making mum as comfortable as possible towards the end of her life. Christmas was quickly approaching, and the kids were excited because their school was having a Christmas concert, and Mum was determined to come one last time. She loved every minute of it, and we loved her being there. At the time, I was experiencing excruciating pain from sciatica that ran from my lower back all the way down the right side of my leg to my foot. I was on very heavy painkillers and could hardly sit still throughout the concert. Even right up to that point, with Mum being as ill as she was, she still worried about how I was instead of about her own wellbeing. Unfortunately, while I was healing, my mum was gradually going downhill. This is the worst feeling in the world, when you cannot do anything to alleviate or stop someone else's pain. It was like a boat on a river, with no rudder, heading towards the edge of a waterfall. Nothing in the world could stop the inevitable. I felt so helpless.

With Christmas upon us the Puppeteer and I decided that this would be the first time in seven years, since we got together, that instead of sharing Christmas with the larger extended family, we would just go away on our own for five days and celebrate Christmas together with our own little family. We did this and we really enjoyed our time away. We came back to Adelaide just in time for New Year's Eve, and as usual, we did not make big plans to go out partying, because Jay was seven years old and Violet was only five, so we ended up going to a friend's house with the kids, had a nice quiet night, and were home by 2am. It was not until the next day that we heard the devastating and life-changing news about a death in the Puppeteer's immediate family that shook and shattered his world and devastated our family. Time stood still, and we were all in denial. Thinking it must have been a mistake. The police must have got it wrong. He was going to turn up and walk through the door, just like he always used to. Unfortunately, it wasn't a mistake. It was the very sad, horrible, heartbreaking, gut-wrenching, life-changing, painful truth, and something that time cannot change.

This was the hardest funeral I have ever been to, and, despite my own mum's ill health; I spread my time to support both families. I know my mum tried to hold on, but five weeks after the Puppeteer's sad news, Mum also sadly passed away. It was one of the worst times in our lives. Despite knowing that it was coming, I really could not have prepared myself for this type of death. I have heard people say that morphine is their friend, but to me, I saw it as the enemy that took my mum's life. I had never heard of the "death rattles", but I swear I will never forget them until the day I die. Cancer is a very cruel disease, and I do not wish it upon anyone.

Life after my mum had passed became very dull. I could not see the beauty in things anymore, and a glaze seemed to come over my eyes that just would not lift. I must admit that I was open to receiving messages from mum from the other side and you really do have to look out for them. They are there if you become aware of your surroundings. Her favourite song would often come on the radio or television, or I would come across her favourite sayings or quotes, and often a love heart would appear in the strangest places. They may seem like meaningless coincidences, but when you are searching for peace of mind that there is something beyond life on Earth, then these signs seem too real to ignore. Mum loved seahorses and had a beautiful collection, so whenever one of these pops up in my world, I know that mum is close by and close in my heart.

After the loss of the Puppeteer's family member and my mum, within weeks of each other, we knew that we had both been dragged through grief and loss to the core of our beings. We were both at our lowest point emotionally in our relationship. I remember saying to him not long after mum died, "Don't leave me, because you are all that I have." He promised me he would not, and I thought he meant it at the time. Slowly, the days turned to weeks and then months, and, as they say, time did seem to heal our hearts, but there was still something missing, and it felt as though nothing could fill the gap or make the pain go away. It was at this exact point in time that, as they say, the enemy took his opportunity to strike and lay temptation across both of our paths. For the Puppeteer it was in the form of a 28-year-old woman and for me it was turning back the clock and going back to the long-forgotten past.

My first suspicions came when the Puppeteer was more than happy to move out into the family caravan, after one of our intense arguments. The caravan was being stored at a friend's place, so it was convenient for the Puppeteer to move into it. This seemed to be working well for both of us for the first fortnight, until I decided to confront the Puppeteer about my suspicions that he was cheating on me. At first, he denied it, but after being repeatedly asked he finally admitted that in fact that was precisely what he had been doing for the previous two months. In that exact moment I was devastated and shattered beyond belief. I was so hurt. I could not believe what I was hearing, and I did not want to believe it. I had so many questions that I really did not need to know the answer to, yet absolutely needed to know the truth, no matter how hurtful it seemed.

Now this whole situation was absolute new ground for me. No one to my knowledge had ever cheated on me before. I had never been on the receiving end of this scenario. Let me tell you, it is not nice. I have been the other woman and have previously felt bad for being in that predicament, but truly nothing in this world could have prepared me or taught me the extent of this pain other than having experienced it firsthand. Thankfully, I did recognise this karmic lesson very quickly and expressed gratitude to the Universe our Ancestors for the experience. For every action there is an equal reaction. For every choice there is a consequence. Despite knowing all the cliches, in that moment I wished that karma and cliches would kindly go and kiss someone else's ass.

Now if only it was that easy and we could move on from this. Life unfortunately is not that simple and when others are involved their speed and level of interpreting their own life lessons or karma may well be vastly different and slower than your own. Without doubt the hardest part that we both found was the rebuilding of the trust in the relationship. Throughout our relationship we both felt that trust was one of the strengths of the partnership. Therefore, before it was broken it was easy for our trust to be secretly broken as neither of us was in fear of the other breaking that trust. Unfortunately, with this comes the heavy penalty, which in the end destroyed our relationship as we just could not ever regain that original level of trust. Everyone that I have talked to have all said that "trust" is everything in a relationship and I believe this to be true.

I remember the exact time and date in 2020 that I decided that the Puppeteer had pulled my last string. It didn't end in a big fight; in fact, it fizzled out like a struck match that burnt its way to the very end. I was at the end of my tether. I was the one who was completely burnt out. And when you know, you know. That's the exact moment when I made a new decision, a new choice, and walked away, never to turn back. The Puppeteer had lost complete control of me and my life. At that exact point, I found freedom.

Throughout this whole puppet-on-a-string experience, I was very conscious of, and expecting, karma to kick in and "pay me back" for what I perceived as my wrongdoings. As a result, I needed to really think about and analyse what my beliefs around karma were. I wanted to be guaranteed that if there was the slightest chance that there could be any benefit whatsoever from the past sixteen years, then I might gain something positive from what felt like nothing but a negative and painful experience.

My basic understanding is that karma results from one's actions. It does not matter whether the action is believed to be positive or negative; the implications of that action must flow on as an energetic exchange resulting in a consequence. Therefore, a balancing of energy is inevitable, just like the balancing of scales. Everything has a cause, which triggers an equally responsive effect. I used to love quoting, "what comes around goes around," with a wicked twinkle in my eye, but with the shoe on the other foot, it was time for it to boot me up the bum. So yes, I did know that cosmic balancing of energy would occur because of the choices I had made. These consequences may come in a variety of forms. It would be easy to describe them as punishments or rewards, but, in fact, karma is not a punishment, it's not revenge, it's not justice. Karma is the Universe and our Ancestors giving you opportunities to alter your actions, revisit your life lessons, review your behaviours and ultimately choose to increase your vibration from low to high. It's an opportunity to do things differently. It is an opportunity to revisit a situation with a fresh set of eyes — a new perspective. It is an opportunity to make different choices and feel how someone else felt. My feeling is that the way we interpret or perceive the whole situation will also determine how we perceive the resulting outcome. Not for one minute do I think that karma is instantaneous. It may well take years to come back around. This is because God, the Ancestors, or whatever you call your Higher Being or Power, uses our experiences as opportunities for us to learn. It's like watching a play in which we are the main characters, and the plot is our lives. Often, during a usually painful situation, the lessons aren't learnt straight away. Often, our level of readiness and openness to learning has not peaked. We are very unconscious of these life lessons. We are nowhere near ready to piece together the puzzle, join the dots, or recognise the similarities to earlier situations that we've either personally experienced or seen close family or friends experience. In this instance, karma may lie dormant, waiting like a lion watching its prey, waiting for the perfect moment to seize the opportunity to grab your attention. Once again, it's not always negative; it often "just is". Everything happens for a reason, and usually at the perfect time. It's what some people call "God's perfect plan". It's only when we look back that we can recognise the similarities to other events in our lives and benefit from the lesson or blessing. This is known as awareness, and raising our individual and group awareness, or consciousness, is one of the main purposes of our lives as humans. It's a hard concept to understand. It's really something that must be experienced, rather than reading about. Once you shift from having the knowledge, to experiencing it, to putting it into practice, and then understanding what just happened, that is when you have raised your consciousness. To experience consciousness in its simplest form is to focus your knowingness and awareness on being fully present, right now in this exact moment, because now is all that there is, or ever will be. Consciousness is the recognition of self and the ability to simply "be." To be able to step out of the chaos, block out all the noise of life, quieten that inner chitter-chatter, and connect with that innermost loving part of yourself, which is consciousness, or God, or divine energy, or ultimately love, what I've come to know as the joy within.

This most recent karmic experience of being cheated on prepared me to shift into the next phase of my life's journey, but I must admit that I wasn't in a hurry for another life lesson, as big as that one, preferably for many years to come.

This experience gave me the opportunity to practice what I preach and put into action the lessons that I had learnt. My life became like a book. It was the book of life, with rules that I continuously forgot and had to be reminded of. It's like I had amnesia, and I needed to be constantly reminded of these life lessons, or rules to live by, from all different sources throughout my life. These lessons came from interactions with people such as my parents, teachers, friends, family, children, society, bosses, and nature itself. I didn't know if I was winning, because most of the time it felt like I was failing daily. Which is what the Bible reminds us: that we are all sinners. We are also all human, even though some of us have worked out that we are spiritual beings having a human experience. And it's hard! This school of life is tough stuff.

Despite life sometimes being tough, and us sometimes feeling isolated and lonely, we do have more things in common than we have differences. However, differences make us individuals, and that's okay. This just reminds us that everyone is growing at different stages in their lives, some faster and some slower than others. Some of us humans understand and work this thing we call "life" out quickly, whereas some are stuck on the clueless roundabout, making the same mistakes as though we are trapped in a repetitive loop. Yet despite our human differences, there are also many similarities. Our lives are very interconnected, and a common thread ties us all together. That thread is what we know as love, or consciousness, and it is interwoven into our universal fabric. Love is what connects us, and it is fear that tears us apart.

Consciousness is not something we 'have' — it is what we are. It is the silent awareness that exists before identity, before thought, before the story of "me and you". At that level, there is no separation, only connection, because we are of the same source. Love, in its original state and purest form, is not an emotion as we as humans generally know and accept it, but the natural quality of simply "being". Fear is simply what arises when we forget who we are, when we fall back into separation, survival, and illusion. Every emotional act of violence, shame, domination, or abandonment begins with forgetting. Every free-flowing act of compassion, courage, and forgiveness begins with remembering.

I realised it was time for me to reflect upon everything that had happened in my life up to this point, take stock, and realign my future path and decisions. Ultimately, I had to move out of my own egotistical way and begin to remember who I was — or who I am.

Equipped only with my thinking mind, I tried to make sense of a pattern of behaviour that made no sense. On the surface, it became very clear that the common thread was abandonment. My birth mum left and lost me, my brothers and sister left this world before me, I left my husband, and when I went to Darwin, I abandoned my eldest son, my best friends and Stolen Generations sisters Mary and Trish left me behind when they went home to heaven. My stepdad, mum and then dad all died and abandoned me like an orphan. This left me relying on the Puppeteer for love. For the sake of my own mental health and wellbeing, I knew I couldn't cope with the fear of being abandoned again, so I left him, and my youngest kids became his new puppets, resulting in me abandoning them, and them abandoning me for a short time, which felt like an eternity

I wasn't consciously aware of this pattern or theme at the time, but once I saw what was going on it helped me to reflect on my life and helped me to realise that I couldn't rely on others for love. If I was going to survive in this world, then I needed to draw love from deep within myself.

I was so busy asking, seeking, chasing, wishing, dreaming, wanting, yearning, and willing others to love me, that, in all of this, I had forgotten how to love myself. I forgot that I am love, and that love is the fabric and energy within that flows between us and arises within us when we allow it to flow naturally. I realised I'd forgotten who I was and lost connection with the deepest, most sacred part of my soul. I'd lost my way, and I had to relearn how to go within and reconnect with who I really was. Somehow, over the years, something on Earth had stopped and blocked me from finding the joy within. That something was fear! The ultimate illusion of life itself.

Once I realised this, I also realised that all this time of soul-searching, trying to find my identity, and trying to discover, "Who am I?" I already knew who I was. I'd never really forgotten. How could I have forgotten? So why was I searching so hard for the answers that I already knew, and had always known? I discovered that I wasn't on a journey to find out "Who am I?", but was in fact undertaking a quest to remember, "who I am."

PART TWO: Soul Searching

Chapter 10
The Truth Beneath My Skin

Over the years, my search for identity has undoubtedly resulted in life patterns of which I am thankfully now more aware. These patterns, or negative core-belief systems, are themes in my life that have either guided or pulled me in different directions. They have been a combination of positive and negative emotions that have strongly driven the decisions that I have made. Simply by writing this book, it has helped me stumbled across these patterns and core beliefs. One thing that I've learnt is that it's easy to see patterns play out in other people's lives, yet it's like we are blind to our own patterns. These negative core beliefs that I've slowly become more aware of in my own life are the good old feeling of abandonment — everybody leaves me, I don't fit in, I don't belong. Then there's the feeling of guilt — I'm bad, I'm not good enough, I'm unlovable — nobody loves me, everybody hates me, I'm dumb, and I need to be perfect.

It has taken fifty years for me to identify some of these limiting core beliefs. I knew that, if I was going to make the most of this life, then I had to challenge these beliefs and find new, healthy ways to overcome them and rewrite the narrative. There's a saying: "If things don't change, then things don't change." Ain't that the truth. I knew it was time to change, and I also knew that with every change in life there inevitably comes a choice, followed by a consequence. When we realise that the only thing we have control of during this challenging time of change is our own thinking, which affects our choices, we may then see the clear connection as to why we made certain decisions. Often, in times of darkness, we are unable to see a brighter future, so we make some shady choices.

Through years of personal evaluation and self-development, I have been able to take a good look at my life and sift through the rubble and the false stories I told myself, which felt like obstacles I've had to overcome. I also reflected on how I turned these into stepping-stones. It was through this exploration and emotional processing that I was able to clearly see my life patterns, which were being driven by my negative core beliefs.

When I viewed my life on a timeline, the first thing that I noticed was that I had achieved so many things over the course of my life, especially during my younger years. I had finished my schooling right up to Year Twelve, then went on to study at university, got a job, got married, travelled overseas, had a baby, had two more babies, and completed more study at university. These were the external things that I thought were positive achievements in my life. These were the things my ego believed made me "successful and happy." These achievements fed my positive core beliefs, like "I am persistent", "I am confident", and "I'm successful". However, these achievements were being driven by fear of confirming a false story and identity that I'd grown up believing I'd become. These positive achievements, unfortunately, weren't being driven by self-love. They were driven by the fear of society and by, "What do others think of me?" Totally unconscious, ego-driven behaviour.

At the time of my self-exploration, I had no idea about the ego. I was soon to discover that the ego is part of our subconscious mind, the part of our identity that we subconsciously consider to be "self". Our ego becomes the thing that determines who we are and how we interact in the world. It's the main thing that shapes our identity. There are both positive and negative aspects of ego, and the key is to balance those characteristics and be a genuine, authentic, healthy, well-balanced human. It's about generating your own sense of internal recognition and not relying on the external world to validate your sense of existence. Or, simply put, not waiting on the world or others to determine your sense of self-worth, or who you are. I finally realised that life is a constant juggle and struggle, based on what society wants to label us with. The challenge is becoming aware of this social dilemma, challenging it, and learning how to be the real you and be happy with that. The real goal is to stay true to the real you. Digging deep, connecting, and remembering who you really are.

When I looked back at the times of crisis or struggle in my life, I recognised that the first major crisis was my separation from my birth mum. Despite always knowing that I was adopted, labelling this event as a crisis or a trauma, as an adult, was confronting. I certainly didn't understand at the time that there is trauma with a little "t", which refers to repeatedly distressing events that cause ongoing significant emotional damage. Then there are the big "T" traumas, which are seen as life-threatening events that cause immediate and severe psychological distress. However, not many people realise that repeated exposure to ongoing little "t" traumas can cause more emotional harm than exposure to a single big "T" trauma. I came to realise that my life was full of a combination of both little and big traumas. So, it is not hard to determine where the "I'm unlovable" negative self-belief grew from. Society teaches us whether these stories are good or bad. So, like a bunch of building blocks, our memories are filtered accordingly, either positively or negatively, which then informs our ego to subconsciously sort and store those emotional experiences. These become our core memories and often shape our personality, also described as our identity.

The next trauma I experienced was when I was six years old, and that's where the humiliation, shame, guilt, and "I'm bad" false story comes from. Then, at nine years old, I was told that my birth mother had died, which only further confirmed that "everyone leaves and abandons me". This belief reinforced the "I'm not good enough" and "nobody loves me" thinking pattern. At the age of fourteen, my adoptive parents divorced, which I thought had something to do with me, so this negative belief ploughed a deeper neural pathway, reiterating that "I'm bad and I'm the problem." The next major challenge was when I was twenty-four years old, gave birth to my first son, and had a postpartum puerperal psychotic episode. I realised that having Jordan was a major achievement in my life, but at the same time, the psychotic episode turned my life upside down. The main themes that came out at this time were "I'm not perfect", "I'm not a good mum", and "I'm dumb". As a new mum, I couldn't cope with not knowing what to do, or how to do this new task of looking after a baby. It wasn't something I could take a test for. I was just thrown, like all new parents, into the deep end of parenthood and just had to learn to be that new parent. However, with thoughts of "I'm not good enough", "I'm bad", "I'm dumb", "I'm unlovable", and "it's my fault", all rumbling around in my mind, I was heading into an inevitable psychological storm. It wasn't until years later that I realised that I'd recreated my birth mothers' story: "I'm not a good mum." This would play out its cruel path in my mind for many years. The next crisis to hit was when I was nearly twenty-eight years old, when Jordan's father and I separated and later divorced, confirming once again to my inner negative self that "everyone always leaves me." After a sixteen-year break, my pattern of pushing away those I love the most reappeared. By this stage, I had decided that it's best to abandon someone before they abandon me. So, instead of "everyone leaves me" rearing its ugly head, I regained control of the situation and left them first. Who would have known that twenty years later at the age of forty-eight, I would end my relationship with the Puppeteer, Jay and Violet's father. I knew that if I was going to psychologically survive this life, then I was really going to have to question these negative self-beliefs: I'm bad, I'm not good enough, I'm unlovable, I'm a terrible mum, I don't fit in, I don't belong, I'm dumb, and I must be perfect or no one will love me. I knew it was high time to find the true joy within.

It became extremely clear that often, after a major achievement in my life, I would soon have another crisis or drama. I was also very aware that I felt like I was following similar behaviour patterns to those of my adoptive mum and my birth mother. One time, I was speaking with a girlfriend, and she brought to my attention that, as humans, we do tend to follow the life patterns of our same-sex parent. In my situation, I have followed strands of both my birth mother's and adoptive mother's life paths, particularly in the romantic relationships department. The other aspect of this untested theory is that females tend to seek partners who reflect their father's traits, and males tend to seek partners who reflect their mother's traits. These behaviours are certainly worth analysing, to see if you are repeating any of your parents' past behaviour patterns. It's a gift if you are already aware of these behavioural patterns, however, often, we cruise through life, completely blind to any life patterns or similarities. Often unconsciously stumbling from one dysfunctional situation to another, while wondering what's life all about, and why we keep falling in love with the same type of person, with the same negative traits, only to realise that it is the same situation and personality, just wrapped in a different human.

I remember, a few years after I'd ended my marriage, when my mental health was at a real low point and my self-esteem was at rock bottom; my older birth brother Bob came over to Adelaide from Canberra for work. At the time, I was divorced and living in the "toxic relationship" with someone who, in my brothers' words, was "not my kind." Yes, he was Aboriginal, which at the time was all I was looking for, but that was about where the bar, and the qualities, ended. I remember my brother pulling me aside and saying to me, "Joy, you know you don't have to make the same mistakes that our mum made." At the time, I just brushed it off, but it truly hit me later, when I got out of that toxic relationship. I realised that while gripped in that unhealthy relationship, I really couldn't see what I was doing to myself. Sadly, many humans are like that. It takes people who really care about and know us well, to point these painful facts out and shake some sense into us. We are so blinded that we just don't want to listen, and we think that we know best. It is when we don't take notice of these small whisperings, that life steps in and presents us with an unavoidable challenge that makes us stop in our tracks and take notice. My advice is to listen to the small voice within, because it will help you find your way out. Also trust that your family, friends and loved ones know you well, and can see things that you can't, and don't want to see. Usually, they also aren't afraid to say it. Bless them!

After nearly forty years of learning these same lessons, I felt like I had gained a new sense of wisdom, so it came as a bit of a surprise that, despite feeling young, I was gradually getting older and, surprisingly, getting a bit wiser along the way. I remember that, at the age of twenty, one of the qualities in life that I wanted to develop further was "wisdom." I must admit that, at the time, I truly didn't have any concept that "wisdom" isn't a skill that can be bought, or even learnt through a textbook. It only comes through life experiences, struggles, and most importantly, time! I now understand that the older we get, the wiser we grow, funny about that! It's such a simple concept, yet it took me fifty years to understand — it's not rocket science! If you look at it from that perspective, it is the perfect example of how wisdom slowly creeps up on us and beautifully reveals itself. It also is true to say that, when the student is ready, the teacher will appear. And as time goes by, what is true will be revealed, and what is fake will fade away. I must admit that even as I'm writing this book and doing the final edits, it's like a light switch is being turned on, and I can see all the common threads and themes that have been woven through my life, and it's like, reading back over my life, I can now finally stitch all the pieces back together. I'm hoping that, after reading this book, it will stimulate you to think about your life, and work out what things keep showing up as life lessons, and, if you're willing to listen to life's whispers, you can use this new learning to help write a new life story, or at least a few new chapters.

I acknowledge that I am nowhere near as wise as I hope to be, but I feel as though I have learnt a few essential and valuable lessons along the way. There is an endless supply of wisdom right within us, that we can call upon whenever we choose to do so. It's just a matter of making the time and space to explore those wise spaces from within. That deep wise space inside yourself is the space where you will find the joy within.

I now know that life does have a real purpose, and it is through understanding what purpose your life brings that you can go on to gain the most out of this thing we call life.

I was lucky enough to work out my life's purpose early in life. I know that everything I do is about loving, healing, and educating others. Not everyone works out their purpose that easily. Often, people just don't know what their purpose is. They feel like they don't have a purpose, or they have no idea how to discover their purpose. What I've discovered is that, when we are working out our purpose, we need to look at our past. Our past often holds the key to the things we feel most passionate about. Our passion or purpose is usually driven by wanting justice, or by wanting to help others not go through what we have gone through. Our passions are often inspired by our personal struggles. When I had my postpartum episode, I continuously asked, "Why me?" When you're in the depths of the crisis, you have no idea what the purpose, or what benefit, can come from such an incident. It's only upon reflection that you will discover what qualities in life this experience will help you gain. In my case, it shaped me into the passionate perinatal health expert that I now am. Unfortunately, most people will remain too resentful, angry, and hurt, and this emotional interpretation of the seemingly negative experience blinds them to the potential learning opportunity it is presenting. At this point, you may well miss your chance to work out what your purpose in life is. When you become emotionally stuck, and living in a time that we have no control over — the past — it continues to control our current thoughts and behaviours, and steals our attention from the current moment — the present. When you are trapped in the past, you lose any focus on the present or the future. This is when we are driven by anger and fear, instead of love, joy, and happiness. We do and say things that we don't mean, and leave an angry trail of hurt, destruction, and damaged souls. As they say, hurt people hurt people. Once we discover our purpose, it helps us to process and release our pain, gives it meaning, and helps us to create beautiful outcomes for other souls. You'll also notice that often our purpose involves being purposeful towards others. When we help others, it helps us find happiness within, that quiet, peaceful space within, which in effect helps the world around us. It helps to positively feed the ego. It takes away our competitive, dog-eat-dog attitude to the world. It reminds us that we are one, instead of separate. It gives us something to get up for in the morning. It gives us a reason for being. That's why we are called human "beings", not human doings. You can only ever "be" in the moment, which is always right now. Not tomorrow, which is the future; not yesterday which is the past; but right here, right now — the present. The only moment that there ever is: "Now!". It reminds us of who we are and why we are all here. Not just me, not just you, but all of us.

To move forward from this overwhelming need to continually explore the past, and be constantly worried about the future, it takes a substantial amount of energy to retrain and redirect our thoughts into a more positive, peaceful space. This takes a heightened sense of awareness. It is like an out-of-body experience, looking from the outside in, without judgement. It is only after we have seen it from this distanced perspective that we are consciously able to be fully present, live in the moment, and make intentional and purposeful decisions. It's like being a silent witness to our own thinking. Watching our thoughts like a hawk! Re-evaluating and reprocessing the memory from an adult's point of view, rather than from a child's perspective. To lock in the new learning, we often need to challenge not only our memory, trapped in our minds, but also the physical sensations that have been deeply buried in our bodies. If our traumatic experience meant that we were unable to run, then, once this memory resurfaces, we need the ability to do what we couldn't do during the time of crisis. We need to physically express the emotions that were suppressed by fear. We need to elicit the opposite reaction. We need to reclaim our power in what felt like a very powerless and helpless situation. So, finding any activity that helps us feel strong, both physically and emotionally, will help to rewire our brains to believe that we are now safe and that the event is over. Finished, and we are renewed. It is when we gain the ability to use our mind, body, and spirit to evaluate our emotional response to any given circumstance that we will find the joy within.

All the people who are angry at past policies or actions continue to relive, and place blame upon, something over which we have no control, and can't change those past actions, experiences, or memories. This is spiritually damaging and only continues to feed the feelings of anger, hopelessness, helplessness, despair, grief, and ultimately fear. In this space of thoughts and actions, we are frozen in time and powerless. It is not a healthy space in which to remain. It is an addictive cycle that lives off its own negative energy, giving back only more anger and pain in return.

I know that in the past I felt angry and held Aboriginal history and past governments and policies responsible and as the source of all my problems, pain and sadness. I knew that this wasn't a good place to be, and I wanted to learn about, and understand, the cause of this anger. I knew that, to get to the root of this problem, which I likened to the roots of a tree, I needed to dig deep, where all growth begins. I then realised that this would mean going back to the past, and questioned whether this would be productive. I reverted to my knowledge of science, and, as with all living organisms, I believed that it comes down to your genetic make-up, which comes from your ancestors. Or does it? That is the question!

In humans, there is an ongoing debate called nature versus nurture. As an adopted person, you can imagine that I can see both sides of this argument.

I do know that there are things, such as the way I look, laugh, and sound, which I have inherited from my birth family, thereby supporting the nature argument. Yet I also know that I have learnt many of my mannerisms, traits, and ways of being, because of the environment and people I grew up around. This supports the nurture side of the debate. It is through a combination of these aspects that various traits, like my attitudes, emotions, and values, have been shaped.

Most people think that I am a quiet, placid person, and few know that when I get wound-up, watch out. You may think that this is an inherited trait from my birth mum. My brother Bob's dad told him that our mum "could fight like a thrasher." On the other hand, my adoptive mum was quite placid, and rarely angered, preferring to avoid confronting situations altogether.

I cannot be sure where all the attributes that make up a unique "me" come from, but I do know that I am a product of my birth family and their genetic traits. However, I have also learnt a great deal of behaviour and thinking from my adoptive family.

Often, we don't realise that it is easy to understand why we are the way we are, simply by looking back at where we have been and where we have come from. We are who we are today, because of our past histories. We have often ended up where we are, because of where we have lived, and from whom we have learnt our behaviours. This point doesn't give you a licence to blame everything and everyone from your past. It is simply a signpost that highlights that we are often a product of the people and environments to which we have been most exposed throughout our lives. I began to realise that, despite being unable to change my past, I was able to decide the future through the choices I made. It also highlights that we don't know what we don't know, and we can't teach what we haven't been taught. Yet, once we do understand this concept, we often immediately look to blame our parents as the source of our problems. Many people believe that we need to lay the blame where it belongs.

As children, we don't have any control over the circumstances in which we find ourselves. Often, when things haven't been perfect, it's easy to blame everyone for our past. My advice is: don't blame others, like your parents, for doing whatever it was that they did, or didn't do, in your childhood. Parenthood is not an easy gig, and, unfortunately, babies, toddlers, and teenagers do not come with an instruction manual! And in the hospital, they also don't hand out a first-time-parent handbook that has all the rules of parenthood. So, rather than thinking about all the "mistakes" your parents have made, remember that they are mistakes only if you don't learn from them. Remember that our parents could only do what they knew how to do at the time. It might help you to ask yourself: how did they learn to do what they do? This brings us back to the roots, fruit, or seeds of the family tree. That's right, they learnt from their parents, and from the environment in which their parents grew up, - and the cycle repeats itself.

To really begin to understand who I was, I realised that I really didn't know anything about my birth mum's past, her mum's past, or my family's past. The only thing that I had to go by was the black history that all Aboriginal Australians of that era were being oppressed and subjected to. My grandparents were born in the late 1800s and grew up on cattle stations and missions, which were places known to expose Aboriginal people to prolonged, cruel, unjust treatment, and the excessive use of power. It really doesn't take many generations of oppression to demolish a community's sense of self-worth and purpose. Oppressors — or, in Australia, the colonisers — knew the art of war. Like domestic-violence perpetrators, who abuse their sense of power and control, oppressors rely on systematic racist policies, backed by legislation in the form of various Acts, to legally endorse their inappropriate use of power and control. The legacy of those outdated policies has carried over even to this day. A slanderous 'othering' hate campaign, driven by propaganda and driving an emotional wedge between the oppressor and the oppressed, was, let's say, unwittingly undertaken. This hate breeds, feeds, and justifies the mistreatment of the 'other', purely based on racial differences. I learnt the word 'ethnocentrism' while studying at university. I'd never heard of it prior to that, and not really given it much thought until later in life. Ethnocentrism is the attitude that one's own cultural group, ethnicity, or nationality is superior to another's. If you can generate enough gossip and hatred towards an entire nation of people, then a stereotypical view of an entire race of people begins to become entrenched and normalised. Even other immigrants to this country have been granted a greater respect and status than our own First Nations people. Newcomers to our land are immediately indoctrinated and turned against Aboriginal people of this country. This gives newcomers a sense of privilege and power in their new homelands, while, unbeknown to them, crushing the equal rights and spirits of the Traditional Owners of this country. After years and years of this insidious discrimination, this behaviour becomes normalised and accepted within society. These inequalities lead to exclusion, and unfair and unjust treatment, among a minority of people. This drives a wedge through society, which often predestines the oppressed person's socioeconomic status, mainly based on race. This is known as systemic racism. In other countries there are class systems, such as lower, middle, and upper class. Which means that you may be born with fewer opportunities, but with sheer grit and grind you can make something of yourself and move out of that class later in life through education and employment. Then there is the caste system, in countries like India, which is based on heritage or ancestry. Most Australians wouldn't believe that we have different classes, and most certainly not castes. However, this country cannot deny that, in over two hundred years of settlement, and since the later establishment of Federal Parliament in 1901, there have only ever been fifteen Aboriginal members of Federal Parliament, as of 2025. On average, there have been 120 members of Federal Parliament every term, every three years, for the past 123 years. This works out to approximately 4,920 Federal politicians over that 123-year period. If you do the maths, only 0.3 per cent — not even 1 per cent — of those politicians have been Aboriginal. It is easy to see how, either consciously and purposefully, or, if I'm being naïve, unconsciously and unintentionally, over 123 years of laws, policies, and practices that appear to be non-biased, have mainly been written by the dominant group of people, who are only mildly affected by the implementation of those laws. Hence, the term discrimination is born. Unfair or unequal treatment of individuals or groups, based on characteristics such as sex, age, disability, sexual orientation and so on. In Australia, most discrimination has been based purely on race — the race of the First Nations people of this country. Aboriginal people have been treated differently, and the system continues to support these prejudiced behaviours. We, as Aboriginal people, have become the minority and foreigners in our own land. Land that was stolen, and whose sovereignty was never ceded. The land was taken by force, and has been retained by force. Which explains why, at significant Aboriginal events or rallies, you will hear the words "Always was, always will be Aboriginal land" repeatedly chanted. Basically, Aboriginal people never legally or formally gave up our land. The colonisers justified, amongst themselves, that the land was "terra nullius" — belonging to no one. The fact that Aboriginal people were already here, and had been for more than 60,000 years, defies that false colonial claim. By stealing our land, dispossessing us from our traditional lands, and stopping our seasonal movements, this immediately ended our ability to survive sustainably. The land is our mother, our source of everything. Once you take away a food supply, people are forced to depend on another source: the government This dependency gives birth to learned helplessness. Despite one's efforts to fight the system, individual efforts become pointless, and you begin to believe you are powerless and have no control, so why bother trying any more? This is where the battle is won by the oppressor. Now you have an entire race and population of defeated, oppressed, depressed, helpless, and hopeless people. Aboriginal people's traditional way of survival and life has been completely compromised and controlled. There seemed to be no hope. No future, no help, no solution. Everything that we once did, as the oldest living culture in the world, has been prohibited and annihilated. Our traditional lores, language, and customs were forbidden, stolen and forgotten. We were 'forcibly assimilated'. Outnumbered and slaughtered. An unadulterated act of genocide. Intentional killings, across over 438 massacre sites where at least 10,000 Aboriginal people were deliberately killed, with the intent to eradicate every Aboriginal person within given regions. So, for the oppressed First Nations people of Australia, there was no choice. It was systematic in nature, legally written into policies like the Aborigines Protection Act, from the 1830s to the 1970s. This gave government officials the authority to determine where Aboriginal people could live, work and be. Most sadly, it gave those in authority the power to legally remove light-skinned Aboriginal children from their parents and place them in homes and institutions, where they were made to work from very young ages. This was supposedly in the best interests of the child, but, truth be known, it was without question, even according to the United Nations (UN) Convention, an act of genocide. An attempt to breed out a race of people. Aboriginal men, women, and children were denied the right to speak their languages and practise their cultural ceremonies, rituals, and rites of passage. Once you lose your culture, you lose your identity and your sense of belonging. You lose yourself. You don't know who you are. Without culture, we have no cohesive society. When we become disbanded, disconnected, separated, and isolated, we are most vulnerable. Without culture, we have no cohesion. We can't practice our cultural ways, which involve the sharing of our rules, or lores, reminding us of our cultural ways of living and providing societal order. Anarchy reigned amongst us, and the oppressor sat back smiling, watching as a race of people self-imploded, carrying out the self-destructive behaviour of the emotionally broken, traumatised, oppressed, colonised black people. Disapprovingly shaking their heads, wondering what's wrong with these people, instead of asking what's happened to these people. There was no remorse. No feelings of guilt or shame. There was no empathy, or sense of urgency, to help those less fortunate. It was as though the entire country of Australia became the colosseum, and the privileged were witnessing the bloodbaths of the era.

We were a beaten people, and instead of pulling together and unifying in the most important fight of our lives, we have been strategically conquered and divided, in typical tyrannical style, weakening any possible resistance among the groups. We were intentionally dispossessed and displaced, causing fighting among our own traditional nations of people. We were made dependent on the colonisers for all our basic needs. We'd never needed money before, but now we had to beg, borrow, or steal to survive. We were treated like slaves, often working as domestics or station hands for no pay, in our own land. We feared for our own lives if we stepped out of line. The only fighting we did was for our own survival. We became a broken people. We fell into line. We were looking for answers, and many gravitated to "religion" as the answer to our sorrows. Others turned to liquid spirits, which lead to further self-induced destruction.

Once I unpacked this historical timeline, it was as though a light came on. It was no wonder I didn't know who I was. I was fighting a lifelong colonial battle that had started well before I was born. Yet the fallout, like a nuclear bomb, was still having its detrimental ramifications for my life, and the life of every other Aboriginal person in this country.

Being a product of this assimilated and discriminatory system, I grew up blissfully unaware of this horrendous history. It now makes sense why I felt indescribably angry for the first thirty years of my life, and why I became very depressed. I didn't know why I wanted to end my life. I wanted to die on numerous occasions. Not knowing who I was cut deeply into my soul. I didn't have the historical knowledge, understanding, or words to describe, or link, my poor mental health to this nation's black history. I know that sounds like a victim mentality, but how could I be a victim, when I didn't even understand, or know, what was being done to me and to all First Nations people of this country? There was nothing of which I was aware, against which I could compare my situation. Feeling like victims, many Aboriginal people forever feel hopeless and helpless, and have a deep sense of self-hatred, yet, in fact, that hatred is more external than internal. It is almost palpable, yet invisible at the same time. It's as though we have been walking around in a world that is continuously gaslighting us, making us think we are going crazy. So, despite Australia signing the International Convention on the Elimination of All Forms of Racial Discrimination (ICERD) in 1975, to protect Aboriginal people from being treated badly because of their race or ethnicity. Perhaps some of Australia's citizens didn't get the memo. So, from that point on, perhaps overt, straight-out racism became more like covert, subtle, undercover racism. No matter what measures are put in place, racism was, and still is, evident and present, perhaps just less explicit and openly displayed.

So, despite feeling hopeless for over two centuries, and believing that nothing will ever change, Aboriginal people are some of the most resilient peoples I have ever known. These strands of hope are what turns victim of crime from survivors to thrivers. This is what we are reclaiming. We take a negative situation and don't let it get the better of us. We have a fighting spirit. Despite being continuously knocked down, we get up one more time. We won't accept our fate. Whereas someone who has a sense of learned helplessness has, slowly over a long period of time, been marinated and negatively indoctrinated into feeling hopeless and helpless. Nothing they do to change their circumstances, or escape their situation, ever has any positive effect. They lose all sense of hope. They feel completely powerless and stop trying and give up. They can't see a different future, so no longer bother to try. It is undeniable that we, as Aboriginal people, have all been exposed to ongoing traumas, however, our degree of resilience and persistence is the point of difference. Our ability to either survive or thrive is what distinguishes us from each other within our shared experience of trauma. I chose to thrive!

I've come to understand that depression is simply anger turned inwards, or suppressed and pushed down so far that you don't let your emotions out, so you are constantly feeling under pressure. Now, the mere mention of the word depression often causes people to cringe. It is something that is common in the community, yet there is still stigma attached to it. I would be surprised if depression hasn't already crossed your own path. If depression has not affected you personally; I am sure that you have family or friends, or you know someone, who has had depression.

Depression ruled my life between the age of twenty and thirty, and I was full of blame and shame for everything and everyone outside myself. I took no responsibility for my feelings, and I felt that I had the right to be angry and sad. I didn't realise at the time that, in doing this, I was giving away my personal power and feeding depression, making it stronger, and making the true me feel weaker and powerless. Sometimes depression can get so strong that it can control your whole life and affect every decision you make. This leaves you in a very lonely, isolated, dark place, that feels like a deep hole with no light, no hope, no future, and no purpose for living. Sadly, for some people, depression drives them to make decisions and choices that end their life in a split second, through an action that sadly can't be undone. This sad example highlights why it is so important that we learn to take control of our thinking, which impacts how we feel and, if left uncontrolled, influences the way we act and what we do. If we let our brain take control of our thoughts, those thoughts can sometimes overwhelm us to the point of no return. We need to learn how to listen to our thoughts, recognise how they are making us feel, and become aware of what emotions they are stirring up inside us. Once we become aware of this, we can teach ourselves not to be overwhelmed and driven to madness, to the point of no return. This is known as emotional regulation. Many people don't know that this is a skill gradually taught throughout our lives, especially during childhood. It is not something that we are born with. If you didn't have a safe person in your life who could calmly respond to your emotional needs when you were overwhelmed, you will go through life like a ticking time bomb. Every overwhelming moment will often lead to angry explosions, the need to emotionally withdraw, and feelings of anxiety, isolation, and ultimately being misunderstood. Unfortunately, this is the beginning of the cycle of intergenerational trauma, which often leads to more disturbing mental-health diagnosis and labels. Depression, sadly, being the least troublesome.

It has only been through a lifetime of experiences, growth, and learning that I have gained a clearer picture of depression. I have found that it likes to play out its role, and fulfil its purpose through your life and the lives of other individuals in this world. You may be thinking: what possible purpose does a nasty thing like depression have? Well, it certainly grabs your attention; it makes you take notice of your thoughts. It makes you take stock of what's really happening in your life. Whether we acknowledge this is the question.

You may have noticed that I write about depression in the third person. I am doing this quite deliberately because I want to draw your attention to a secret that I have come to learn, which will help you to break free from the social and emotional labels, bonds, and diagnoses that so many health professionals love to label you with, according to the DSM-5 (Diagnostic and Statistical Manual of Mental Disorders), which is like the diagnosis bible for a psychologist or psychiatrist.

The key to escaping from the grasp of depression, and any other disorder, is to disidentify yourself from it. As soon as you begin to believe that it is part of who you are, it becomes like poison ivy that grows out of control, overtakes your mind, and strangles your thoughts. By identifying with it, it affects the way you think, feel, act, and do things in your daily life.

How often have you heard yourself, or someone else, say, "I have depression," or "I am depressed"? My advice to you is to become aware of what you are really saying! By saying you have depression, what you are really saying is that depression is no longer just depression; now you are depression. and depression is part of who you are. You and depression become inseparable; you are it. and it is you. You are one. This becomes your identity. This is a dangerous headspace to be in.

If you want to end this identity crisis, you must set yourself free from it. Start to create a new, stronger, healthier identity for yourself. I promise you: you will find a new you that you never previously believed existed. Enough of being controlled by what others have negatively taught us, or indoctrinated us, to think and believe about ourselves. No more self-limiting negative self-beliefs. Challenge every harsh word from your past, and challenge those lies. Reinvent yourself, become who you've always wanted to become, and be the best you that you can be. Ask yourself, "Is what they've said about me true, or is that just what they wanted me to believe," so they could control and manipulate me, and feel better about themselves? Just like all oppressors and manipulators do.

It may seem to you that I am just playing with words; however, our subconscious mind works in a very word-sensitive manner. It believes everything it hears, and then acts accordingly. It can't tell the difference between what you say and what you believe. Remember, if you say that you are depressed, then your mind acts according to your words, which then become your beliefs, which become your life. The best way is to change the way you think is to change the words you use, and the way that you use them. Dr. Wayne W. Dyer (2009), author of The Shift: Taking Your Life from Ambition to Meaning, has a great expression that also explains this concept. "When we change the way we look at things, the things we look at change." Or, in more recent times, Joe Dispenza reminds us to "pay attention to your personality, because it becomes your personal reality". That's powerful. Reclaim your power!

Now I know that my name, Joy Makepeace, draws attention and comments, but despite the "by name, by nature" comments, in my early twenties I was often struck with deep bouts of depression and found getting out of the sadness and feeling of hopelessness was crippling at times. These were the times when, although I was obviously loved by too many people to name, I experienced such deep depression that I thought my world was closing in on me and believed that no one loved me, or would even miss me, if I were to end my life. I felt so alone and lonely that I didn't want to live. This type of depression and desperation can be understood only by someone who has been to the bottomless pit of despair. If you are someone who has not experienced this turmoil of emotions, count your blessings and never wish this experience even upon your enemies. It is such a dark place, from which suicide often seems the only solution. Let me tell you, it isn't the solution. So, I am hoping that these words may toss a lifeline to you, or someone you know, who is presently in that dark place.

Over the years, I have come to believe that depression really is unresolved anger, and beneath anger is unconscious fear. What I've also discovered is that, when we are angry with others and seek revenge for their wrongdoings, it is like the old Chinese proverb that says, "We drink a bottle of poison and expect them to die." Through depression, we are attempting to reclaim control of our lives, but in this unhealthy way, we are only hurting ourselves. Take the time now to say the following words out aloud, and let your spirit and soul hear them. "If I truly love who I am, why would I turn my anger inwards and be angry at myself?" And here, once again, lies the key. Self-love. When we don't truly love ourselves, the opposite shines through. Self-hate. When we hate ourselves, this is when we become angry with the world, and are full of anger, blame, shame, and guilt. This is when we begin to point our fingers outwards, instead of turning our eyes inwards and look within our souls to find the answers that have troubled us our entire lives. If you're feeling overwhelmed and have no ideas where to start, I recommend becoming mindful. This is the opposite to what it sounds like. Having a full mind is not the goal. Being mindful is a skill that you need to develop, which will help you become an outside witness to your own thoughts and feelings, which are usually responsible for your emotional reactions. It is like being a hawk, flying above your thoughts and watching where they come from. It is also about becoming consciously aware of that natural internal chatter that incessantly and relentlessly goes on and on and on in our minds. It's about taking back control of your mind. It is about not allowing it to control you. It's about recognising that you are not that voice, which really is the ego within us, that identifies with everything that has ever happened to us and has a conditioned belief system that hijacks our thinking, unless we become aware of it and stop it in its tracks.

If left unattended, our ego thinks it is doing us a favour by being so smart, protective, and self-important. The ego thinks it can intervene at the first sign of trouble, and urges us to be deeply offended and protect ourselves. However, our ego thinks it knows what's best for us, based on its survival memories. It calls upon these seemingly protective strategies that have helped us get through things in the past. Sometimes those strategies worked, but often they are dysfunctional ways of surviving very scary situations. Often our egos are remembering a situation over which we had no control, and one that needed a certain protective strategy to get us out of a distressing predicament. Often, these decisions we make in times of crisis are reactive, not responsive. The difference is that being responsive means you've thought things through and can guess the possible outcome, but being reactive involves little to no thought. It's a survival instinct. When no thought is given, there is also no thought given about how the situation is going to end up, or to the consequences of your actions. It's usually after the fact that we can think, "Maybe I should have, or could have, done this or done that." Yet we know consciously that we didn't, and that becomes shameful, and when we are ashamed that we didn't do something to change the outcome of a situation, we become powerless, feel helpless and hopeless, and become angry. Yet we still don't, won't, or can't do anything to change the situation. We become apathetic — showing little or no interest, concern, or emotion — which also sounds as though we are being "pathetic". To feel pathetic is debilitating. It's that learned helplessness raising its ugly head. It's the choir of negative voices that remind you of everything that you are not. They are convincing and consistent. When you are in that position, it feels like you have the weight of the world on your shoulders, and there's no way out. It's like being a rat on a wheel; you have run yourself in circles only to realise you're getting nowhere. You feel that you are still as powerless today as you were yesterday. Nothing is changing, so why bother. Why even try? It's not worth it. "It" becomes you, and you now believe you're not worth it. You believe you are worthless. You give up!

This is a very hard pill to swallow when we are faced with what seems like the truth. We end up either denying or suppressing our anger, which turns to depression. It is those unexpressed, forgotten, subconscious memories that remain buried for years. Yet, secretly, our subconscious, our emotions, and our bodies remember. These hidden memories fester inside us, often presenting as physical pain in our bodies. They remember every hormonal and chemical response that our body reacts to, and experiences, with every uncomfortable instant of our lives. It codes the experience in a secret message, immediately labelling it as our feelings, and later, often more long term, as our emotions. Whenever we get triggered by one of our senses — like what we are seeing, smelling, hearing, tasting, or touching — our memory is instantly unlocked, and usually our bodies also distinctly remember an incident that is like the current traumatic situation, which triggers our emotional coded memories. In that instant, we make a choice either to become aware of it and try to process it, or to decide it's too overwhelming, and choose to remain justifiably hurt, angry, numb, and we rebury it. We try desperately to control the pain. Sometimes we shut right down and dissociate (mentally escape), which is our brain's way of taking a much-needed break to cope with the perceived threat. Until we find healthy ways of revisiting these traumatic memories, the unresolved pain lies dormant in our bodies, temporarily forgotten, just waiting for the perfect emotional storm to erupt again. It really doesn't have to be this way, but it is very confronting to declare that you want to change the way you feel, and don't know where, or how, to start. This takes time — between the actual event and the much later adult recognition that something bad happened, and you repressed it to survive it. Most of these memories are from a time when we were very vulnerable child. To emotionally revisit this deeply stored long-term memory is extremely frightening, and I recommend that you seek professional help to re-explore those memories in a safe way, and find a healthy way to gather all the pieces of the puzzle from an adult perspective and put them all back together from a new, higher, more mature, and interpretive self-perspective. It is only from this wider viewpoint that we can rewrite our history and see the situation with new eyes. It's like putting on a new set of glasses, with a new set of frames. Maybe this is what they mean by reframing the situation. It's also the perfect opportunity to tell the truth. Truth-telling is healing! Being seen, being heard, and being believed is relieving. It allows us to regain our power and control. It brings back our strength. It rewrites the story. It helps to create a new you.

This next insight that I want to share with you did not come to me overnight. It is a very emotional issue, and may be one that you just simply are not at the point of accepting. I must admit that I was tightly bound to this identity, to the point of self-destruction. It has taken deep soul-searching, time, effort, counselling, and self-exploration to get myself to this new point of understanding. This new knowledge has had the greatest impact upon my healing journey, but it was something that I had to discover for myself. Therefore, I am hesitant to even mention this subject to you in this written form. I hope that you will be open to this next lesson, but please understand that it is my perspective, and I also value and respect your individual journey.

As an Aboriginal person, I strongly identified with this nameless force that had drastically influenced my life up to that point. I believed that my feelings were rightly justified, and I felt as though I had many stories of despair that continued to feed the source of my pain. At the time, I did not realise that it was a legacy and identity that had been handed down to me through at least two generations, by way of an endless supply of both conscious and unconscious sources.

It may seem like I am making no sense at all right now, but what I am talking about is my obsession or addiction, that dominated my thoughts and controlled my life. I don't want to just blurt it out; I really want you to work this point out for yourself. It will have more impact this way. Perhaps I've made you think that, in my earlier years, I was addicted to something. Well, figuratively speaking, I was, but it was not a narcotic or hallucinogenic drug. However, it was something that met an unfilled need within me: the need to know "who am I?" I just had to know who I was. I was prepared to do, and be, anything to meet that need. The only way that I knew how to contact who I thought I was, was to get back in touch with the identity to which I had attached myself.

So! I hear you are screaming out to me: if it wasn't drugs that you were addicted to, what was your addiction? What was it that filled the void inside you and made you feel whole again? What was it that made you feel better, and made your feel like you belonged?

Once again, the answer was simple: I was at my happiest when I was with my mates Vic and Tim, being a vic-tim. Yes, that's right: being a victim was my addiction. Without even being aware of my behaviour, I genuinely thought, felt, and acted like I was a victim of past policies, and believed that I had every right to feel that way. I was angry, I was hurt, I was depressed, I was guilty, I was bitter, I was jealous, I was envious, I was resentful, I was unforgiving, I was unhappy, I was lost, and at the core of it all, I was full of fear! I justified my behaviour and my existence through my Aboriginality. It was my birth right to be all those things, and it made me feel as though I belonged. By holding on to this identity and anger, I believed I was a "real" Aboriginal person.

In this sacred place of victimhood, I was able to seek refuge with so many other lost souls. It became an identity to which I unknowingly became attached, and with which I deeply began to relate to and resonate. For the first time in my life, I felt accepted, and felt a sense of belonging. All of these were genuine needs that I was crying out to have fulfilled. It's easy to now see why I felt so comfortable being in that place of acceptance, and why I became so strongly attached to that identity for so long. It not only met my identity needs, but I willingly fed the needs of other too, as we licked our painful wounds together.

What I didn't realise at the time was that I had dramatically restricted my own growth; I was self-sabotaging my life's journey because I thought I had reached my destination of finally knowing who I was. In this place of victimhood, I thought that I had found my identity and discovered who I was. When, in fact, what I had done was give my power away again. Instead of becoming self-determined, I had become a victim of my own poison, and a bitter product of past policies that wanted to define me, control me, and ultimately identify and assimilate me. Instead of becoming empowered, I had given away my own power. I was labelled and tagged by a society that showed no respect of who I really was, or where I had come from physically, spiritually, or emotionally.

I can remember the exact moment that the penny dropped in my conscious mind, when I realised that I was not a victim! I was thirty-eight years old, and it was my fifth visit to a female counsellor whom I'd been seeing through my workplace Employee Assistance Program. Over the earlier visits, I am sure my counsellor and I had covered a range of topics and areas of own concern to me, and for the first three visits, I had told her all the reasons why the world was against me, and why I blamed everyone else for my problems. My finger was, without doubt, pointed outwards at the world and everyone in it. I took no responsibility whatsoever for my own suffering. It was all out there. It was all someone else's fault. It was being done to me.

Now, as a good counsellor, she empathetically listened to all my feelings and reflected back to me everything that I told her, for which I was extremely grateful. This made me feel like she understood where I was coming from. I felt that she felt my pain and understood the injustices that I'd been served. She was so good that I even thought she agreed with me.

However, somewhere in this entire process, with the wonderful skills of this counsellor, I slowly started to take responsibility for my own thinking, feelings, and actions. I know that at the time I was completely unaware of this shift in thinking, but before I was even aware of what I was doing, I must have stopped blaming others and started to use the word "I" a lot. I can't remember the exact words, but I must have said something like, "I'm not a victim." Suddenly, this female counsellor got all excited and had a grin from ear to ear; she was practically bouncing out of her chair. To be completely honest, at the time, I didn't even realise what the fuss was all about. I truly wasn't even aware of the importance of what I had just said, or what had just happened, or what I had taken responsibility for. I wasn't aware because this newly discovered knowledge had not yet truly filtered from my subconscious into my conscious awareness. What I'd done in that session, without even realising it, was take responsibility for my past feelings and take back control of my future happiness. I regained and reclaimed my personal power — my destiny. I was no longer at the whim of what others thought of me. I was the boss of my brain. I was the captain of my ship. I can now recognise why it was such a momentous occasion. Some people never get an insight like this in a lifetime. And here I was, breaking my own personal best record. It surely was a golden-buzzer moment.

Later that night, the Puppeteer and I were out on an evening drive. I decided to tell him what had happened earlier the day in my counselling session. It was a bit weird because, as I started to explain it to him, it was like somewhere deep within myself, my soul was listening to the echoing voice retelling the story of my discovery that I was no longer a victim. I heard myself telling him how, all this time, I had believed it was everyone else's fault that my life was the way it was, but in fact, I hadn't realised that all this time I had been in complete control of my life, and I'd been the driver of my victimhood bus. The more I explained my session, the more excited I became, then suddenly. Then, suddenly, I found myself bouncing up and down in the car seat, just like the counsellor had earlier in the day. It was in that exact moment that I knew why she had been so excited.

To learn that I was not a victim, and that is not who I was, or who I am, or who I want to be, was the most amazing feeling I have ever felt. It was a major "aha" moment. It has forever changed my life. At first it was liberating to know that I no longer had to carry around that identity, but then, upon this realisation, it became very confronting and exposing. It had been my identity for so long, and I honestly believed that was "who I was." When I discovered that this wasn't the case, I knew then that I had to review my life all over again. I had to find out who "I" was again. I was now free to "be" the real me.

All the attached angry, hurt, resentful, and bitter emotions immediately melted away and I stopped blaming others and felt empowered by this newfound knowledge. I suddenly realised that I was in control of my mind, my thoughts, and my life. It was the most healing moment I had ever had in my entire life. It was the turning point of my life, and I have never looked back! Being a victim was my addiction. Having discovered that I no longer needed my daily fix of bitterness, anger, or blame, I now feel like a reformed alcoholic. I was no longer addicted to being a victim. I knew this was the start of a new way of thinking and being. It was a new lease on life.

As with all addictions, I am aware that I am constantly susceptible to relapse and, in this case, to feeling like a victim, so I am extra careful of whom I surround myself with, and what I read or watch on television. I choose to surround myself with positive people, and look for uplifting experiences and environments. I have finally discovered that, if you want to change, you must change yourself, and only then can you be the change you desire. As they say, if nothing changes, nothing changes.

Some people believe that life is just like a bed of roses, and I often wondered how this could be, when I used to feel as though my life was like a bed of nails. I have since realised that those that think life is like a bed of roses must have been wearing rose-coloured glasses, which makes it easier to see life that way. I've also come to realise that the bed of nails is still there, but when you begin to think about life in a different way, and block out that bed of nails with the help of rose-coloured glasses, orpositive thoughts, then life will always smell, or be, so much sweeter.

I remind myself daily that, in our lives, we are continuously challenged and exposed to circumstances that may seem incredibly sad and often debilitating. It is during those moments, when we are most vulnerable and want to catch up with our old mates Vic and Tim; that one of these moments for all of us is most definitely when we experience grief and loss. Grief and loss test us all. It calls upon every one of us to draw strength from a healing source that is deep within us, but it is often so hard to find that it escapes us.

There is a world full of textbooks, self-help books, websites, pamphlets, and courses that try to explain what grief and loss is, and how we can better cope with it. When we are right in the depths of grief and loss, we don't want to hear, or read about, someone else's interpretation of how we should "get over it." Grief is an extremely personal thing, and one that is not always easy to talk about. It can affect every cell in our body, and every aspect of our lives — if we let it. I say, "if we let it," hesitantly, because I know that it is like saying, "just get over it."

I can almost hear you saying, "What would you know about grief? You weren't the one that experienced the loss, you aren't the one who has been left behind, you aren't the one that has to continue living my life." To all these statements, I agree. To help explain how I came to my new understanding of grief, I want to share an experience that I had when talking to someone about the loss of a dear friend of mine. At the time, I did not realise that this experience would dramatically change my thinking, which in turn changed the way I now feel about grief. It has also changed my whole belief system and my behaviour surrounding, grief, loss, and death.

I remember when I lost a dear girlfriend of twenty years to cancer; from diagnosis to the day that she died, it was a six-week period; so, in terms of time, it was quick. As you can imagine, I was experiencing all the usual emotions associated with grief and loss, such as denial, anger, disbelief, and depression, and was feeling quite shocked and empty on the inside. To try and help release my own suffering, I innocently wanted to share my feelings with another friend. Sometimes, when we talk to others about our loss, it seems to help. I started to explain to her about how sad I was feeling, and how shocked I was because this disease had taken my dear friend so quickly. To my absolute and complete surprise, the lady that I was talking to said, "Oh, how wonderful!" Well, I never! Blow me down with a feather. My jaw nearly dropped to the floor. I couldn't believe how shallow and disrespectful this woman was being towards me. I can tell you my offended ego felt instant anger at her lack of compassion and empathy towards my feelings, towards me, and towards my friend. Yet right there, in that moment in time, was a lesson to be learnt about perspective. Life is always about how we look at things, and it is depending on how we perceive them that we manage to move forward through the situation and manage our emotions. What this lady had done was take the emotion out of the situation and see it for the natural transition from life to death that it was. She didn't know my beautiful friend, and therefore had no attached emotions that selfishly wanted to keep my friend here on Earth with me. She saw the situation for what it was: a girlfriend who was in a lot of emotional and physical pain and suffering, and who was ready to go home, to Heaven, quickly — and that's what she did. With this quick transition, it was all over in the blink of an eye. It wasn't drawn out; it just happened quickly, and the family could then let go of the pain they were carrying while watching their mother, sister, and aunty go through this transition, going home to her beloved God and returning to the light.

Unbeknown to me at the time, what this lady had unwittingly used was a well-renowned psychology technique I referred to earlier, called "reframing." It's a term that doesn't really resonate too well among people because, once again, it means that we must, as the old saying goes, "change our frame of mind." This is an extremely awkward thing for people to do because often it's the only way that we have been brought up to think. It seems almost disrespectful to move on emotionally with our lives too quickly after the death of a loved one. It's as if we need to honour their memory through the depth and length of our sorrow. This distorted approach to grief and loss has becomes a part of who we are, and it becomes part of our identity, and we hold onto our sadness for years, honouring our loved one's memory. Keeping their memory alive through our grief seems as though that's the only sense of hope left in such a sad situation. Unfortunately, this way of dealing with grief and loss keeps us stuck, suspended in time, and most certainly stunts our spiritual growth. Reframing helps us look at the situation from another angle. It's another way life teaches us a lesson, and helps us look at a situation from an alternative perspective. Would your loved one have wanted your life the cease just because theirs did? I didn't think so. They'd want you to live your life like there's no tomorrow. Keep dancing until the music stops. Fulfil all those dreams that you shared together, and enjoy every moment like it's your last. Hold onto the positive memories, and let go of the pain. They want to reassure us that they are no longer in pain; they have returned to paradise, which is where we all go when we've had enough of this life. They want you to live the life that they couldn't.

Quite often, life's lessons aren't exactly clear to us straight away, and it's a bit like a scene from the TV show "Days of our Lives", where the sand passes through the hourglass. Life's lessons have a way of gradually filtering information from one level of our consciousness to the deeper levels of our subconscious. Hopefully, with this comes an awakening, and an aha moment, or "enlightenment", which sheds light on a situation. To define enlightenment is like asking how big the sky is. There is no definitive answer. It is a knowing within; it's the realisation that we know nothing, yet we have always known everything. So, knowing that what we have always been searching for is not outside of us, but within ourselves, is a big step towards enlightenment. There is no travelled, proven route to enlightenment. It is an individual path that every one of us is unconsciously travelling. Some are just more aware that they are seeking it faster than others, and the Universe, our Ancestors, know it's not a race. However, it starts with the humble beginnings of love and has no ending, and it is what everything is made of. It is the ability to accept that there is no right or wrong, as you open your heart, mind, body, and soul to infinite perspectives; therefore there is no one truth. It is about letting go of all that you thought enlightenment was, and instead of chasing it, allowing it to unfold and reveal itself to you. It's about losing all attachment to anything physical, and merging into nothingness while being everything all at the same time. It's something that must be found deep within your own soul, which is ultimately where you find the joy within.

Do Not Weep

Do not stand at my grave and forever weep.

I am not there; I do not sleep.

I am a thousand winds that blow.

I am the diamond glints on snow.

I am the sunlight on ripened grain.

I am the gentle autumn's rain.

When you awaken in the morning's hush

I am the swift uplifting rush

Of quiet birds in circled flight.

I am the soft stars that shine at night.

Do not stand at my grave and forever cry.

I am not there. I did not die.

-Author unknown-

Chapter 11
Heart of the Matter

Life gives us numerous examples of how our world has two halves that join to make one whole. Evidence of this surrounds us daily; it's just that we have become so immune to the simple beauty of life that we forget to notice these basic principles in nature. Some say that we live in a world of duality. A world full of opposites that we see daily, such as night and day, north and south, east and west, black and white, left and right, and yes and no. This list of opposites often presents us with endless choices. As you go through your day, I want you to become more aware of all the wonderful choices and opportunities we are endlessly given. And remember, perhaps it's not one or the other; perhaps you can find meaning by embracing both sides of the literal coin. If we didn't have the dark, we couldn't appreciate the light.

Often, we think that we have no choice, and no control over the circumstances we find ourselves in. In fact, we do have control over everything, and the one thing that we can take complete responsibility for is our choice of how we respond or react to others and to situations. We can simply choose to either be calm or angry, positive or negative, happy or sad. Is this true or false?

There are no right or wrong choices in life; there are simply consequences. I am sure that you have already made choices in your lives, as I have. I am often asked: would you have changed anything from your past? In years gone by, I would have jumped at the chance to say, "Yes, of course I would make different choices." Now I don't regret the choices that I have made because, undoubtedly, they have helped to shape me into the person I have become. These are the lessons I was destined to learn. Don't give away your sense of power and feel that life is just steering you in the wrong direction, because you are the captain of your ship, and you set the course of your future through the choices you make. Remember, whichever choice you make is simply another chance for growth, which helps you continue learning more about yourself and life.

Whenever the opportunity to make a choice comes along, always think about where you have come from and where are you going, but most importantly, think about what the best choice for you is right now! And where do you think this choice is most likely to lead you? Who will the choice most influence, and is it in line with your values, passion, and purpose?

I wish I had been given this next simple piece of advice years ago, because it is the key to all achievements in life. It is also something that we all know, yet we all forget its importance. It's a simple principle, and it can help you achieve absolutely anything you want in life. As with everything in life, there is a catch — it only works if you use it!

This principle has only just become blatantly obvious to me. It is something that we all know, yet we rarely stop to think about the impact of its potential. I promise you that anyone who has ever succeeded at anything, big or small, in life has, without doubt, used this principle. It is impossible to achieve success without it.

Over the years, I have read endless amounts of self-help books, yet it took me twenty years, to finally discover this principle, acknowledge it, embrace it, and now use it to its full potential. When you finally "get it", it will slap you in the face, and you will be kicking yourself that it has taken so long for this information to register in your mind. Once your mind understands and decides to act, it filters down to your heart and then moves into your bones. Your bones and muscles then move your body so that you can take the necessary actions you've decided upon, which makes the things you want to achieve, happen!

This principle is an important part of the web of life. It is tangled up with all the other life principles and cannot be separated. I want you to remember that, once you think about something you want to do, then decide that you will do it, and then let it settle into your heart, you will begin to feel the burning desire to do it. You see it with your mind's eye. You feel it with every sense in your body. This encourages your body to generate the energy it needs; this is when you decide to take the necessary actions required to achieve it.

Believe me, once you have mastered this principle, there is no turning back. You will be thanking me all the way to the bank, and in fact anywhere else you decide to drive your life. Just decide to be persistent, and never ever quit! If you have read this whole chapter and still have not got what the principle is, just decide to go back and read it again and again until you do get it, because it is written right here before your eyes, and you need to decide never to give up until you have found it.

Never Quit

When things go wrong, as they sometimes will,

When the road you're trudging seems all uphill,

When the funds are low and the debts are high,

And you want to smile, but you have to sigh,

When care is pressing your down a bit,

Rest, if you must, but do not quit.

Life is strange with its twists and turns,

As every one of us sometimes learns,

And many a failure turns about,

When one might have won had they stuck it out.

Don't give up though the pace seems slow

You may succeed with another blow.

Often the goal is nearer than,

It seems to a faint and faltering man,

Often the struggler has given up,

When they might have captured the victor's cup,

And they learnt too late when the night slipped down,

How close they were to the golden crown.

Success is failure turned inside out—

The silver tint of the clouds of doubt,

And you never can tell how close you are,

It may be near when it seems so far,

So, stick to the fight when you're hardest hit—

It's when things seem worst that you must not quit.

-Anonymous-

The last principle was about deciding, and consistently and persistently making that choice. This next principle is about using your willpower to achieve it. It's about resisting temptations, and using a lot of self-control. Now we might have heard the term "willpower", but do you really know what willpower is? You will often hear people talk about other people who are strong-willed. What does it mean? In my mind, it means people who are self-determined, people who get things done, people who take initiative, and are the ones who are successful, achieve things, and never give up. This is the positive side of being strong-willed, or having a lot of willpower. As with everything in life, there a flip side. There are strong-willed people who can be controlling, egotistical, pushy, bossy, and arrogant — yet they still get things done and achieve what they want, usually at the cost of others. This is not a path I recommend. This is when the negative side of the ego is unbalanced.

The path you decide to take, about the use of your "will", is up to you. My only advice is that there are no right or wrong answers; there are only choices. The "will" that I want to talk about is associated with your mind, but it is not your thinking mind. It is deeper than that; it is part of your subconscious mind. Once again, it is a simple term, yet one that holds deep meaning and requires adequate appreciation and understanding.

Your "will" is like a muscle, and the more you learn to use and control it, the stronger it gets. If this is the case, then the opposite must also be true. The less you use it, the weaker it becomes. Just like muscles, you need to train yourself to develop, build, and grow your "will" power. This can be practised with all the simple decisions and choices that we make daily. It is a matter of us beginning to become aware of the constant choices that are available to us, and becoming consciously aware of the decisions we make based on those choices.

Next time you are trying to decide what to drink, such as tea, coffee, orange juice, water, or even an alcoholic drink, just decide to make a conscious choice. I "will" have a coffee, please! Say it with a determination that lets your mind know that you are standing strong in this decision. You are the captain of this ship. Should I sit down and relax and watch television, or "will" I take the dog for a walk? Should I do the washing, or "will" I visit a friend? As you can imagine, the choices are endless and ever-present. It's just up to you to grab hold of every opportunity and steer your life in the direction you want it to take, not the other way round. The bottom line is, our "will" is always present, and we are free to make different choices, so there is truth in the saying, "where there's a 'will' there's a way!" However, a word of precaution: with every choice comes a consequence. Be willing to accept that too.

This next principle occurred to me one day when I was driving along in my car, off in a mindless world of my own, as we often tend to do. I was not really concentrating on the present, or living in the moment. At that specific moment, a golden-coloured Holden Commodore caught my attention. It had bright yellow words stuck on the back window. The words that caught my attention were, "Faith is stronger than fear!" Now, if you are anything like me, you may see this as a literal sign. It was so significant and relevant that it demanded my attention and begged me to obey the message. I repeated the words over and over in my mind, and I read the sign over and over. I wanted the message to trickle down from my thinking mind into my knowing heart. The more I read it, the more it began to ring true. I started to realise that, yes, faith is a matter of "what I believe I can achieve", and fear is simply false evidence appearing real. So, if fear isn't real, then follow faith. Often, we want to have so much control over everything that goes on in our lives that we forget that sometimes you just must go beyond believing, and "let go and let God." This is usually extremely hard to do, especially when we are being strongly driven by our ego and are in such desperate need of control.

I wondered to myself: what was the sign trying to tell me? I think that it was highlighting the fact that so often you set goals and have great intentions, yet despite knowing that you have all the things that you need to succeed, secretly in your heart and your mind you still don't truly believe that you can achieve it. This sign is a constant reminder to overcome your fears and have faith that everything is in Divine order, so yes, "Faith is stronger than fear!"

Now this final, and most important, key to life is about gratitude. Thank you, thank you, and thank you again. How often in your life have you given thanks for what you have? How often do we worry about all the things that we don't have, instead of being grateful for the things that we do have? Do you have a lack of appreciation for the wonderful things you already have in your life? Sometimes life just passes us by, and we don't even take a minute to remember and acknowledge the simple things in life. Then you start to jump up and down and wonder why life is so hard, and why everyone else seem to be the lucky ones in life.

Throughout my life, there have been times when I have been extremely grateful for individual things. However, it has only been quite recently that I have begun to really take notice of both the small and big things I'm grateful for, and start to say thank you to the Universe, our Ancestors, for bringing these wonderful things and opportunities into my life. Every day, when I wake up in the morning, I thank my Ancestors that I am alive and well! I lie in my bed with my eyes closed and allow all the beautiful thoughts of gratitude to float into my mind, and I consciously acknowledge them and say thank you. At the end of the day, I often write down all the things for which I am grateful. I go through my day and give thanks for the wonderful, and not so wonderful experiences I have had throughout my day, and I say thank you for all these experiences, and thank you for the lessons that I have learnt from them.

These can be important things, but often they will be the trivial things in life. You might like to do something as simple as give thanks for all your senses: your ability to see, hear, smell, taste, and touch. I always give thanks for the beautiful people I get to meet and share my life with every day. For this, I know I am blessed.

Next time your day ends and you are lying in bed worrying about what the next day will bring, refocus your thoughts and remember all the wonderful things that you experienced during your day. Give thanks for everything you do have, rather than focusing on worrying about what you don't have. When you truly start to appreciate everything that you already have, and thank the Universe, our Ancestors, for meeting your needs, or even going beyond your wildest dreams, I can guarantee that you will reap the rewards from your efforts. I'm sure you will be pleasantly rewarded for looking at the world through new eyes.

Chapter 12
Wisdom in Pain

Dis-ease! It sounds so nasty. You may notice that I have spelt the word dis-ease with a hyphen. I am not the first person who has done this. The first time I saw this was in Louise Hay's book, "You Can Heal Your Life." Louise's main belief is that "if you are willing to do the mental work, anything can be healed." My beliefs are like those of Louise, and I also believe that our bodies can heal themselves.

If you just take a moment to stop and truly think about the miraculous intelligence of our human bodies, the amazing world that we live in, and how everything precisely works together in harmony, then you must begin to wonder, if everything is so divinely designed, then why do we get sick with dis-ease?

Our mind, body, and spirit can heal us; however, this is only available to those who choose to truly listen to what their body is telling them. As they say, you can lead a horse to water, but you can't make it drink. Even if someone were told everything that they needed to do to make themselves well, unless they follow that advice and make the choice that they want to get well, I would strongly suspect that the dis-ease would persist. The other thing I know is that a person can be very sick, and a traditional healer can see that they are spiritually sick, but unless that person asks for help, the Ngangkari can't or won't do anything to fix them. What you need to understand is that most of our healing comes from the belief and choice that we can be healed, which all begins with our own choice and decision that we want to get well.

People forget that our entire world is made up of bits and pieces that all neatly fit together to form a whole system. Everything is interrelated and connected. Affect one part of an organ or the environment, and in response it affects the complete system. Therefore, it is essential that, when we look at our bodies, we don't just look at the one part that is not feeling or performing well. You must consider the body in a holistic way, which is why many health-related businesses are leaning towards holistic health and healing. Your body gives you constant feedback and messages, letting you know what is right or wrong with it. Unfortunately, we don't take notice of the signs it is giving us. In fact, Western medicine will often give you medicine or a tablet that will make that symptom disappear. That is dangerous. It is a band-aid fix, and it discredits the perfection of our bodies and their internal, natural healing systems. We need to take back responsibility for our own health, and start to become more aware of what our bodies are trying to tell us.

Our bodies speak to us through a variety of ways: pain, tears, temperature, colour, sweat, nausea, diarrhoea, inflammation, and cramps. These are our signposts, or red flags, that show us that something is wrong. They let us know when something is not functioning properly. If we are wise, we will take notice of these signs, and we will at least try to work out what we need to do to fix the problem. Often, we can fix the problem ourselves, and since the introduction of modern medicine we have become reliant upon doctors for all the answers. Instead of taking notice and becoming aware of the signs our bodies are sending us, we want to quickly suppress the symptoms, deaden, and instantly get rid of the pain. No one wants to experience pain, even for a minute.

This works for a short while, but usually a new symptom will appear, trying to grab your attention. We find yet another drug to overcome the new symptom, meanwhile deeply burying the original problem. It's a vicious circle, and it could all be avoided if we take a holistic view of our health. Often, people see themselves as separate bits and pieces, with no other connections. This is so distant from our rich past, and we have disconnected from how our minds, bodies, and spirit need to work together in a balanced way to gain the best out of life. We no longer consider ourselves whole, but instead act like robots without a mind, body, or spirit. We begin to split ourselves into separate organs. Our mind takes care of our thinking and our emotions; our body responds to the physical stimuli that come in through our various senses; and our spirit is the energetic field around and within us, a long-lost, forgotten part of ourselves. Since the beginning of time, we have been created to operate and function as whole beings. It's the same concept as how perfectly the whole universe operates. There are systems within systems. Trees make oxygen, which we need to breath, and without oxygen we die, but we also breath out carbon dioxide, which the plants need to create sugars that feed the tree. As a by-product of that reaction, oxygen is transformed through photosynthesis and released back into the environment. It's a perfect and endless cycle. Each system is reliant upon the other for survival. The same applies to our bodies: we need our lungs to breath in oxygen, which gets diffused into our bloodstream, which travels like a river through our veins, throughout our entire body, and reaching every organ, which is made up of cells that need oxygen to help them grow and break down the food we've eaten to release the energy we need to survive. Even our cars work in a similar way to plants and our bodies. Basically, we add fuel to the car; the fuel and the air, oxygen, mix, creating a small explosion, or energy, within the cylinder. The piston uses that energy to move the crankshaft and other parts that thrust the car into motion. The car emits carbon monoxide; eventually this gas reacts with oxygen in the environment and forms carbon dioxide, and so the cycle of life goes on.

Unfortunately, when it comes to humans, we constantly and repeatedly ignore the signs and symptoms that our body is desperately trying to show us. We totally disrespect our bodies, filling them with toxins, which leads them to breaking down and weakens their natural ability to repair themselves. When we only take into consideration one aspect of our health, you can be guaranteed that we will inevitably be missing vital information that could better help us to heal holistically.

We might feel better for a little while, but the underlying issue is often an emotional cause that goes undetected. If we only address the physical aspects of the dis-ease and ignore the mind and spiritual aspects of our lives, we are missing vital pieces of healing information. It would be like trying to start a car without a battery, fly a plane without an engine, or bake a cake without flour. You need all the right ingredients brought together to ensure it works properly. Of course, things won't work properly if they don't have the right ingredients, or all the parts. Why is it that we continue to punish and abuse our bodies, putting the wrong fuel and food in, then feeling confused as to why our mind, body, and spirit are not in balance, and unable to give us the best performance possible?

If you really want to put your body back at ease, then carefully consider everything that is going on in and around you. Ask yourself, "Am I choosing the best quality ingredients to add to my recipe of life?" Am I surrounding myself with the best people, and is where I am living, working, and spending my time the most nurturing environment for my whole self? Once again, it's your choice. The answers are available, but whether you choose to pay attention or not is the real question.

Now there are always going to be critics in your life. They are full of disapproval, and they often find fault in everyone's behaviour, but never in their own. No one likes being criticised, so why do we criticise others? What does it achieve? Do you honestly believe that it helps people to become all that they can be by telling them all that they are not? I don't know of one person who enjoys being criticised. I don't know anyone who feels that criticism is a positive experience for them, so I am very confused as to how the term "positive criticism" originated, because those two words seem to be as opposite as they can be. I just can't see how the word "positive", being placed before the word "criticism", makes it acceptable and softens the blow. To me, it says that yes, I was feeling "positive" and thinking I was doing all right before you decided to "criticise" me and turn the situation into a negative, yet that's called positive criticism, and I'm supposed to learn from this advice.

It's like when someone tries to soften a hurtful comment with, "I don't like to be mean but….", or "If you don't mind me saying, but….", or "I don't mean to be rude, but…." All these statements lead down the same destructive and hurtful path, which ends in criticism. There is nothing positive or constructive about criticism.

My suggestion is that, if you really want to be positive and constructive, and want to help others achieve their goals and dreams, then avoid criticism. Instead, find the good things that you can talk about, and avoid negative comments. Seek the positive things that someone achieves, and point out their strengths, not their weaknesses.

Often, after we are criticised, we can become bitter and resentful, so in terms of relatedness, these emotions could be cousins to anger. We feel hurt and full of hate when we think someone has done us wrong. We become unforgiving. It is an ego-driven game of shame and blame, and a very hurtful one that can simply eat you up from the inside out.

We want the other person to say "sorry" first, believing that everything will then be all right. Often, the other person is also holding resentment towards us, and thinks that you should say "sorry" first. When we have held onto our resentment for such a long time, sometimes the other person may no longer even be alive, or they may have moved away, and you may never have contact with them again. What happens to you and your body when you hold onto these unresolved feelings and pain? And have no way to get rid of it, or process it? That's right, you become "stuck" in your emotions and tied to your past. What is really stuck is the energy within us. Research suggests that different areas, muscles and cells, of the body store different stuck negative emotions. Anger in the head or chest, disgust in the mouth, sadness in the throat, anxiety in the chest, shame in the face. If you don't shift these emotions, this is when you are most vulnerable to becoming sick. You develop a disease because you are feeling dis-eased.

How do you overcome these feelings of hatred, anger, bitterness, and resentment? This is where the real work begins, because, you guessed it, if it's to be, it's up to me! There are many natural ways that we process these emotions; children are openly good at this first way, which is crying. Crying is very healing. Did you know that emotional tears often contain stress hormones and other substances not found in normal tears, which lubricate our eyes? Another popular way to release our emotions is through talking. Some people love to talk it out; others prefer to physically work it out. Some are more introspective and like to go within. Many of these methods will help you get off your high horse of resentment. It's a bit like our close friends "Vic and Tim", or depression; we start identifying with being "resentful" and "bitter", or a "victim." They become part of our identity. Our ego, which is driven by our emotions, wants to protect us from ever being hurt again. Sometimes we think, if I say "sorry", I will no longer need to feel angry, resentful, or bitter, and then what will I be left with? That's right; you are just left with love and the true you. Gee, I bet that makes you feel like you're standing naked in a room full of strangers, stripped of your angry defences. Yes, it is a big "ASS…K.", pardon the pun, firstly to acknowledge that you are still holding onto "anger, resentment, and bitterness;" then it is an even more challenging to expect you to be the bigger person who says "sorry" first.

The most important thing that I want you to remember, when you decide to say farewell to "anger, resentment, and bitterness", is that it does not mean that you believe what the other person did was okay. What it does mean is that you are choosing to no longer stay connected to them, or to the experience, and you now willingly "let go" of the past, releasing yourself and your memories tied to that event. You have made a positive choice, and you should celebrate that you want to feel free and move forward towards a brighter, stronger, more positive future. This is the beginning of the forgiveness process, which dissolves feelings of guilt, resentment, and blame.

Now there is one disease that we are all familiar with, which also literally takes over your body. It's called cancer.

Often, we never connect the dots, and how dare we even propose that cancer and unforgiveness be associated. Anyone who has lost a loved one to cancer would call bullshit on this statement. But I swear there are clinical studies that show that over 50 per cent of cancer patients have unresolved forgiveness issues. I can say from personal experience that every person whom I've known to die from cancer has had a huge amount of stress, anxiety, and unresolved grief, loss, and pain. Often, before their illness, they were the busiest, most productive people. Yet they can also be the most guarded, defensive, and private people you'll ever meet. Their business is their business. It's too personal to be shared, so it's not to be talked about, it's not ever to see the light of day. It's a secret that remains in the dark. It's never to be remembered. If we don't talk about it, it didn't happen. So, it gets filed away into a cellular memory until one day it decides its showtime. And show up it does. By the time cancer shows up, it really has taken hold and control of your body, and demands your attention. It's gone from a whisper in your ear to something like a megaphone. There's nowhere, and no way, to avoid this health concern. It's action stations, and it's all hands-on deck. What intervention they administer depends on how advanced the diagnosis is. By this stage, the last thing on your mind is forgiveness work. The whole process becomes like a wild horse running out of control. There's no slowing down, and no trying to turn the chaos into calm. It's full of fear, and very rarely can it be stopped.

Now, I have heard of a few, far-between people who've beaten the odds and beaten cancer. But I can also honestly say that they did the work. They heard the message loud and clear, and knew that this was where the rubber hit the road. It was the end of the road, and they had to make a choice. A choice to forgive, a choice to live. It makes sense why everyone thinks that cancer is a very unforgiving dis-ease. It doesn't cost a cent to forgive, but unfortunately it can cost your life if you don't.

You've probably heard of the sayings "dark night of the soul", "it's time to do some soul searching", or "do the inner work". If we must search, it suggests that something is hidden, and that something needs to be found. Something needs to be brought to the light. In fact, it's our soul that needs the light. So how do we find what's being hidden by our subconscious? How do we find out what needs a bit of light shed on the subject? It's not until you discover, what that "something" is, that you have unconsciously been holding onto for years, that you can "let go" of those painful, unforgiving feelings. Now, talk therapies can get you to a certain point of healing, but these memories must be reprocessed and physically let go of, or shifted. Now we can help heal our past by revisiting it in our minds eye, and imagining how we would do it differently. But sometimes, for real healing to occur, we need to physically do what we didn't have the strength or opportunity to do when the "something" happened. So, if you needed to run and you couldn't, then run now. If you needed, or wanted, to punch something, then punch something inanimate now, if you wanted to scream, or yell, or cry, or throw, or break something, then do all of that right now. Get it out of your system. Get it out of your mind, get it out of your thoughts, out of your head, and most importantly, get it out of your body, and finally out of your memories. Let it go, burn it, bury it, give it to the ocean, chuck it in the river, throw it in the rubbish, flush it down the toilet. Do whatever you have to do to be rid of it. But please promise that you will do something. Because it's when we do nothing with something, that something becomes everything.

Now, all those solutions and actions I've just mentioned are the tough approach to forgiveness, which is like pouring bleach on a hard-to-remove stain. However, I promise you there is a softer approach to forgiveness, which is more like pouring fabric softener into the wash. You could write about whatever your "something" was, sing about it, paint about it, breathe deeply, stretch and pray daily, walk mindfully, dance with abandon, laugh until you cry, meditate and contemplate, sit still with it, swim until you're wrinkled, hug it out, massage and/or shake it off, exercise until you're exhausted, or perhaps it needs to be exorcised — be gone. Talk until you can't yarn any more. Do whatever you have to do to release it. Set it free. Forgiveness is like untangling a ball of wool. It can be done, but yes, it takes a lot of patience and persistence. The harder you pull the worse it gets. Sometimes you just need to hand over that big mess to a higher power, saying you've tried, but just can't undo the last knot. None of this forgiven-but-not-forgotten business. Let's deal with it now. Then forget it. Let it go. It's over. It's finished. The end. I swear you will feel lighter, and finally find peace and even some joy within.

In traditional Aboriginal societies, there were lores that determined right from wrong. If you did someone wrong by breaking the lore, then there most certainly was a consequence. The elders determined the punishment for the crime; it was dealt with for all to see. But once it was delivered, it was over, done with, the end of the matter. There was no time for resentment; there was just pure lessons and repercussions to ensure the survival of the mob. Karma was dealt with right then and there. Forgiveness naturally followed. Life went on. It was tough love at its best. People learnt respect, honesty, and ultimately love for one's culture and for each other. The lores ensured safety and a peaceful, just society.

I want to share with you my experience of forgiveness in action. I can honestly say that finding forgiveness in my heart is exactly what happened to me when I attended the National Apology in Canberra, ACT, on the 13th of February 2008. When I heard that the Prime Minister, the Hon. Kevin Rudd MP, was going to make an apology to Australia's Aboriginal and Torres Strait Islander members of the Stolen Generations, I just knew I not only wanted, but also had, to be part of this historically significant event. I arranged to go over and meet up with two of my closest friends, God rest their beautiful souls, who were also "Stolen Generations" women. One of these women was originally from South Australia, and the other was from NT; both had been removed from their birth families. These women had been my soul sisters and support networks for fifteen years before the National Apology.

We had laughed our way through our sorrows, and we had often talked for hours, comparing and sharing our life stories with each other. To have both of my Stolen Generations soul sisters by my side at the National Apology was the most beautiful experience I could have ever asked for.

As we had arranged our own trip to Canberra, we didn't get to sit in the House of Representatives Gallery at Parliament House for the National Apology. Mary, Trish, and I were over the moon that we got to watch the proceedings on big screens set up in the Great Hall. I remember the buzz in the air; Canberra was alive, and the Parliament House grounds were filled with thousands of people. There was a sea of black and white faces, and there were cameras and film crews everywhere. In the air, I could smell the fire of the infamous Aboriginal Tent Embassy, which had been kept burning, against the odds, without permission, defiantly for the past thirty-six years, since January 1972, coincidently the same year I was born. I wondered if a part of me was born in that smoke. Against all odds. That fire, that smoke, filled the air and reminded us of all the undeniable truths, and signified the ongoing fight for Aboriginal Australians' political rights. It felt like the burning desire to know who I was seemed to be reflected in the dancing flames of the fire. It was a truly spiritual and cleansing moment, having my body immersed in the smoke of that spiritually powerful fire.

As we made our way up Capital Hill, as it is known, it felt like a mountain I had been waiting to climb all my life. There were thousands of Aboriginal and Torres Strait Islander people, and other Australians, watching the National Apology on huge screens while sitting on the lawns outside Parliament House. The National Apology was live on every news channel around every state and territory in Australia, and across the world; it was an occasion of national and international significance. I felt like this day was just for me! Yet I know that every other person there also thought it was just for them.

When we walked into the Great Hall, we were directed to sit up the front of the room in a specially roped-off section that was just for members of the "Stolen Generations." For once in my life, I felt like I was special, important, recognised, and honoured for being Stolen Generations, and our pain and suffering were acknowledged, and that we finally belonged. The day was just for us. I will always remember that feeling. As Mary, Trish, and I sat there with our hands interlocked, it was like we had all become little children again. We all waited in anticipation for the big announcement that we had travelled so far to hear. Even though it was only two states away, I knew that I would have travelled to the end of the earth to hear that one word — "Sorry." When the time came for Hon.

Kevin Rudd MP to deliver the main message, you could have heard a pin drop. Silently, the tears flowed, and hearts slowly began to open. Everyone's feelings of guilt, resentment, and blame began to melt away, and the nation's healing process began.

I must admit that I didn't hear everything because my head was spinning and my palms were sweating, but I do remember Hon. Kevin Rudd MP saying,

"For the pain, suffering and hurt of these Stolen Generations, their descendants and for their families left behind, we say sorry."

This is everything that I had ever wanted to hear. This was enough acknowledgement for me. This let me know that I could "let go" of the past and move freely into the future, and it was all that I needed. That day, that word, that moment changed my life! I am forever grateful to Hon. Kevin Rudd MP for fulfilling my hopes and helping me to release myself from my past. It is truly miraculous what forgiveness, and the word "sorry", can do!

Despite my feelings of elation, it became clear that, around the nation, there were thousands of people feeling guilty. Guilt often occurs when our reflective thinking is full of bitterness, resentment, anger, and hatred towards ourselves for having done something that is against our own moral code. Guilt also often occurs when we think that other people are thinking negative things about us. If you were a car, then it would be like a temperature gauge hitting red on your dashboard. This shows you that something is not right. It tells you that you need to stop and check that everything is okay. You need to check your moral compass.

Guilt affects different people in different ways. Often, guilt affects your physical, mental, emotional, and spiritual health. Guilt makes you feel angry, defensive, ashamed, and gives you an overall feeling of depression. When you feel guilty, this is because you're having an internal tug-of-war with your morals, or value system. To help you avoid feeling a sense of guilt, you first need to work out what your values in life are, and what you believe is acceptable and unacceptable behaviour. You need to establish what your line in the sand is. What's your yardstick? What are you measuring your guilt against, or in comparison to? The amount of guilt you feel will depend on how strongly you feel about a certain value. If you think that stealing is wrong, then you will feel extremely guilty if you steal. If you think that lying is wrong, then you will feel guilty when you lie. If others do things that are against your moral belief system, then you will feel that they are guilty, and this triggers a response in you based on the value you believe they've violated.

All these feelings of guilt start to build up like a big pile of rocks that you have thrown into your emotional backpack. They can weigh you down and make your journey through life extremely hard and uncomfortable. How do we remove guilt from our lives and set ourselves free from the invisible ball and chain which guilt punishes us?

Once again, the answer is simple, if only you "will" apply it. Forgiveness is the key. You will only find forgiveness when you seek forgiveness, firstly from yourself, and then from the person whom you have hurt and held responsible for your feelings. For a lasting result, I also suggest that you seek guidance from a source higher than yourself, whatever that may be for you. I've often heard it described as horizontal forgiveness, which is from person to person, or heart to heart, and then vertical forgiveness, from person to source, and in return from source to person, which is more like heart to soul. The feeling of peace will be instant; you will feel as though a weight has been lifted from your shoulders and removed from your emotional backpack, which was once full of rocks. Your emotional temperature gauge, on your internal dashboard, will return to green and normalise to a state of calmness, so you can continue to cruise safely along your journey of life. It doesn't mean that you won't get retriggered by the next similar situation; it just means that, for now, you've acknowledged that it is beyond your current comprehension, and bigger than you understand and can currently deal with. It's also something that you don't need to deal with right here and now. When it's time to revisit this, a situation will undoubtedly present itself again. Seeking forgiveness for something you feel guilty about, or something you think someone else is guilty about, is like asking the Universe, our Ancestors, to help us tap out, like a wrestler does when they are forfeiting the match. It's acknowledging that you don't know the answer, and you no longer want to struggle with this problem. It's time to let it go. Admit temporary defeat, and be okay with that.

Sometimes, along my journey of life, I notice that I begin to feel anxious and fearful. I usually feel most anxious and fearful right before I get angry. A wave of emotions begins to build up inside me. As the conversation goes on, I begin to feel my heart rate rising, my breathing becomes a bit shallow and rapid, my fists curl up and squeeze tight, my thinking starts to race, my thoughts become clouded, and I'm totally distracted. I am completely emotionally dysregulated. This type of anger is like a volcano that's been bubbling beneath the surface and is ready to erupt. With this build-up type of anger, there are warning signs, and you have a split second to respond to a situation rather than react, which is the other explosive type of anger, more like a firecracker. It blasts in the blink of an eye, usually without warning, and often in the middle of a crisis. This is usually a reaction to a dangerous situation when you are scared. This type of anger is driven by absolute fear. You have no time to think logically about your actions, and you simply react.

In the past, reactions like these were humans' inbuilt friend. We needed to rely on them for survival. That is where the term "fight or flight" comes from. You stood your ground and fought for your life, or you took flight and ran to save your life. In this case, your body made a split-second decision, put your safety first, and ensured your survival. You weren't the one making the decisions; your body was reacting before you even knew it.

Next time you can feel yourself getting angry, try to stop and ask yourself, "What am I thinking?" "Where have my thoughts taken me?" "Why is my thinking making me feel angry?" "Am I really feeling angry, or is what I'm thinking about making me feel scared?" "Should I react or respond?" Try to slow down the entire process. Take deep, slow breaths, and count them on the way in and on the way out. Try to control your thinking. Try to be an outside witness to your own thinking. All these actions bring awareness, insight, and light to the situation. Instead of reacting, you have given yourself the time and space to quickly analyse your internal dialogue, or voice, and then respond in an informed, rational way, rather than react in an illogical, irrational, unregulated way. In a calm, rather than angry, way.

When you have worked out that, beneath all the layers of anger, there is a deeply buried hurt or painful feeling, and the thought of it surfacing raises fear from deep within, acknowledging its presence will almost immediately extinguish anger, like a flame going out. By letting go of the anger, you are then able to work through the fear. Anger believes it is doing its job, thinking it's protecting you from exploring the real reason for your emotional unrest. If you can't feel it, you can't heal it. Some people go through an entire lifetime doing anything to avoid feeling any emotions. Numbing their pain with any addiction, both healthy and unhealthy behaviours, that distracts their mind, body, brain, and soul from becoming aware of, or noticing, what's really going on inside their minds. This is when we are mindless instead of mindful. Completely blind to, or unaware of, what's really going on in our minds.

Have you ever been told that you have a big ego? Do you think the people asking you that question really know who you are, and do you think that they are making a correct judgement about you, or do you think that they don't know you at all? And why would they say that? Only you can answer those questions, and if you are thinking "How dare they say that I have a big ego, that's not who I really am," this tells me it is time that you and your ego spent time getting to know each other, and once again it's time to ask yourself, "Who am I?"

When I first started writing this book, I know that I was searching for my identity, and I wanted to know the answer to that same question. Who am I? I didn't realise at the time, but this is a tricky question to answer, and it does take time and years of soul-searching. Other people act as though they know who you are, based on their personal assessment of you and your ego, but do they really know who you are, or who I am? How could they, when I hardly know who I am? To help find the answer to that question, it is necessary to start at the beginning. When I say beginning, I don't mean at the start of this book, or even when or where you were born. What I am referring to is before our mothers, our fathers, or even any of our ancestors were born and walked this Earth. I'm not even talking about, "Where did I come from?" What I am talking about is: "Where did we all come from?" "What are we all made from?" and "Where do we return to?"

Oh, that question! I hear you say. The question to which no one knows the answer, and if they do, then they don't share it because they say it's one that you must discover for yourself. Right about now, you are probably either feeling bored, scared, or outright annoyed at what a waste of money you've made in buying this book. This is a good place to be, because it is another classic example of your ego at play. Ego controls so much of our lives, and is often disguised, and has allies that like to distract us from the truth. The ego is like living a lie, it's the decoy that takes us down a different path, away from the truth. It creates a persona that it wants the world to see you as. It describes you as what you look like, act like, have, do and be like. It feeds on the idea of impressing others with all that you have, both in material trappings and in anything else that demonstrates an ounce of success. It's like the rich Aunty or Uncle who really aren't rich, but want to world to believe they are. The ego is based on deception, and the main person it is deceiving is you yourself. It's all smoke and mirrors — basically trying to hide the truth. What we truly are is far from what the ego wants others to believe about us. Not only does the ego want the rest of the world to believe this illusion, but it also wants to convince us that, without these things, titles, achievements, and attachments, we are worthless. Which, deep down, we know is untrue. What is the truth? Unfortunately, until you have done the necessary internal work, and found the joy within, then this topic will not make sense, as it really needs to be experienced on a spiritual level.

Biologically speaking, we have a body, which is physical. Then we have a mind, which controls our thoughts; our thoughts generate our feelings and emotions, based on our cellular memories and histories. Finally, we have a spirit, which makes us spiritual beings having a human experience. Our spiritual side is the most difficult for people to understand. This is because it is like electricity; you instinctively know that it is there, but it's not something that you can physically see or measure. It is mysterious, and a connection with oneself that needs to be developed, strengthened, and grown. To try and strengthen it you will need to acknowledge that yes, you do have a mind, body, spirit, ego, heart, and soul, but you are not any of these, because you are The Soul, which is an eternal spirit. The part of you that survives death. All that ever was, and all that ever will be. The part of you that is found deep within you. It is the joy within every one of us.

In Aboriginal culture, "kurunpa" is a Pitjantjatjara word for this part of us. It is our spirit, our soul. However, the word kurunpa doesn't even do it justice to what it is. It's much more complex than I can explain. It's a bit like trying to explain what electricity is. Aboriginal people are very spiritually connected to everything. The land is our spiritual mother, and we are born of that. Everything comes from the land, and the land sustains our life. Without the land, or the connection to our land, our spirit, "kurunpa", becomes disconnected and makes us sick. We become unwell. We may even die.

Finding the joy within really is about reconnecting to that sacred part within yourself, and everything that surrounds you. This quiet spiritual way of listening, and being in touch with your spirit, is like a practice called "Dadirri", according to Dr Miriam Rose, or in my Kamilaroi language it is called "Winanga-li". It's about deep listening; it is the inner quiet stillness that helps you to attain a sense of peace, joy, and pure bliss, which helps you to find healing within yourself. If you manage to find this quiet place within, this may very well be the start and finish point in your life, as you know it. You may just realise who you really are! It is an incredibly special moment that answers all questions and explains all; it is a moment to be truly remembered, because you are remembering who and what you are, and where you have come from, and where you will return to. It reminds you that you are not separate, and that we are one with everyone and everything, yet at the same time we are no-thing.

Some people will experience this point of understanding while sitting on top of a mountain like a yogi; others may have an epiphany, or aha moment, while watching a sunset on an isolated beach. I think mine occurred, outside of meditation, the first time that I visited the centre of Australia — Uluru. I felt like a speck of sand in comparison to the size and magnitude of this monolith, which is one of the seven wonders of the world. My life seemed insignificant, and my problems and worries pointless and no-thing in comparison to the big scheme of life. It was deeply spiritual, breathtaking, mesmerising, and mind-blowing. Uluru is a highly sacred site for the Anangu people of the Central Australian desert — the Red Centre. I've never been to Egypt, but in comparison, the Great Pyramid of Giza is apparently less than half the height of Uluru. Uluru is taller than the Eiffel Tower, and over three times taller than the Statue of Liberty. The base of Uluru is 9.4 kilometres, and can take up to 2 hours to walk around.

When and if you get to this place of understanding, you will learn that everything that you and your ego tried to convince you that you were, you are not. There is only one truth, and you will find that the ego wants you to believe the exact opposite.

PART THREE: Finding the Joy Within

Chapter 13
The Way Out Is In

Now, one of the sure ways that I know for you to find the joy within, without having to physically go to the Himalayas or Uluru, is through meditation. I don't want you to get discouraged by the word meditation, because it is just a word! What I want you to concentrate on is how to find that sacred space within.

Our lives are so busy, and we never seem to stop thinking. Meditation is only one way of bringing our mind to a quiet, sacred space. I want you to find whatever it is that helps you get rhythm or repetition on which you can focus, and that takes you away from your usual thought processes. Some people like to do an active meditation, like bush walking, knitting, swimming, gardening, horse riding, bike riding, listening to music, or gazing at the stars, but many meditators prefer to sit in silence. Whether it's active or calm, just be consciously aware that you want to slow down your mental chatter and focus on your simple "beingness." The hot topic of this era is mindfulness. Which, to me, seems counterintuitive, because what we are trying to do is not have a full mind. We are trying to have an empty, clear, and quiet mind when we meditate. Our thoughts often won't stop, so just be mindful and allow non-judgemental observation of your thoughts as they come and go in your mind. Being mindful is the objective, which involves going within and paying attention, but not having any attachment to our inner thoughts. If you don't want a physically active type of meditation, you may wish to lie down and meditate, but some find that this is far too comfortable and tend to immediately fall asleep. If this often happens, perhaps standing or sitting in a comfortable pose may better suit your needs. At the end of the day, being comfortable is the key, and finding a quiet setting where you are least likely to be disturbed. You may listen to someone on YouTube talk you through a meditation session, or you may have gentle music playing in the background. Alternatively, you may simply be listening to your own breath.

I was nineteen years old when I first experienced meditation. I was studying full-time at university, and I knew that I was really stressed out. I didn't really know much about meditation, but I did have a preconceived idea about what its purpose was, and I was hoping that it would take me to a place where all my problems and stresses would be forgotten and left behind. I remember lying there on the gym mat, trying so hard to lie still while I listened to the voice of the facilitator. The harder I tried to lie still and let my mind go off to a faraway place of peace and tranquillity, the more my body just seemed to want to itch, scratch, and wriggle. I never really managed to explore the heights of the open skies, or delve into the depths of the deepest ocean. I just lay there wondering what this meditation thing was, and why everybody swears by it. It just seemed to me that it wasn't all that it was cracked up to be. With this failed experience embedded in my mind, I didn't bother to explore meditation for another seventeen years. I just muddled my way through life like a lone ranger, slaying all my emotional dragons within my own mind. Those years inside my own mind were pretty much like an emotional battlefield within myself.

The next time I was reintroduced to the practice of meditation was in a class session during my post-graduate studies. I was thirty-six years old, and I was more mature and gained a more insightful experience this time. I was able to relax and let go of my immediate surroundings, and I managed to find that sacred space. I finally felt like I had a glimpse of what others had been talking about. It was quite special, and this was the beginning of a truly special ongoing journey. This time I felt like I'd been a bird, and had been able to look at the land below, and really had a bird's-eye view of the world. From this perspective things, started to make more sense.

Whenever I am feeling stressed, or need answers, I find myself using the principles of meditation and go to that sacred space where my mind is still, and my thoughts are clear. It is the unique gift that you can give to yourself. This is where you can have a personal conversation with your Guru of life, God, Ancestors, Divine Being or whatever you call, or use to describe this sacred interaction or relationship. For me, it answered the biggest questions that I have always had. Who am I? And it was in this sacred space that I found the joy within.

After about a year of practising meditation, I finally had an epiphany and reached a place where I felt like I had left this earthly world behind. When I was in my sacred quiet place, I merged into a sea of pure love. I was no longer an individual, I was not even a woman; I just was. I realised we are one! The overwhelming sense of peace and love supplied so many answers to every one of my questions about life, and I remembered who and what I was, and where I had come from, and what my purpose on Earth was. I also knew where I would eventually be returning. In that exact moment, I knew that I wasn't afraid of death because there is no death. I am eternal. Our physical body, that has carried us through life, may be gone, but pure consciousness, pure love, remains forever. When you realise that what we are, and what we have come from, is pure love, and that we are all one and cannot remain separated, it is exhilarating.

I am sure that what I experienced was only one of the many spiritual realms, which will eventually become vividly clear to us once we return to where we have come from — home. This one memorable and very life-impacting experience has stayed with me, and reminds me of who I am, and guides me daily to live my best life. Without a doubt, it is worth the effort to still your mind. I can promise you it is life-changing! But it is like a muscle, and if we don't use it, or practise it, we lose it. So, remember to try to find the joy within every day.

Have you heard the old expression, "Change is as good as a holiday?" This is true, yet we are often so comfortable with the way things are that we are too scared to do anything different. Usually, we end up deciding to stay the same, and keep our lives just how we like them. That's right — "predictable!"

Have you ever attended a conference for a couple of days, and each day found yourself sitting in the exact same spot the whole time? We are just absolute creatures of habit! Every time we walk into that same room, we head straight to the exact seat that we sat in the day before. Why is that? What are we afraid of, or why are we so dependent upon familiarity and predictability?

It takes real effort and willpower to ensure that we "step out of our comfort zone" and choose a different path, or simply a different seat. What happens if, one day, we do decide to sit somewhere else, or take another route home from work, or wear something different from our usual outfit, or get our hair cut differently? Usually, the first thing that happens is that we get a new perspective. This can come just from changing what we normally do. You get to see the whole picture from a new angle, and you gain a new way of seeing the world. By changing the way you do, or look at things, you are changing the balance of energy in the room, and this then shifts your own energy. What you will find, when change occurs, is that a whole new range of opportunities will arise. You might get to meet a new person, and form a new friendship, or you might notice something that you haven't seen before. You might simply realise that your headaches don't come back because you can see the whiteboard without having to twist awkwardly. As Dr Wayne Dyer always said, "when we change the way we look at things, the things we look at change."

Who knows what the outcomes of your decision to make a change may be? Why not make a different choice today? Even if it is a slight change, you must start somewhere. Next time the impulse to change starts nagging in your subconscious, don't ignore it; use your willpower to instigate the change that you want in your life. You just never know what wonderful things are around the corner. Most importantly, remember, "nothing changes if nothing changes."

I truly wish that someone had told me this when I was younger, because I know it would have saved years of fights and stress. Over the years, I know I have been guilty of thinking that I was okay, and it's just everyone around me that needed to change. If only they'd change this or that, then all would be fine. What I have discovered is that other people's behaviour is out of my control. It's taken a while, and I regularly remind myself that you cannot change someone else; the only person that I can change is myself, and the only person you can change is yourself. It took me a good twenty years to realise this one! It seems simple, yet we waste years of energy blaming others and wishing they would change. When you realise that only you can change your life, then you will realise that you are in complete control of your life. If you wait for everyone around you to change, then you are giving away your power and responsibility, and nothing will change.

I promise you, next time you meet a challenge in your life, instead of expecting everyone else to change what they are doing, decide to change what you are doing, and watch how your circumstances improve. It is amazing! It is so empowering, and it works every time. I love it, and it just makes me feel so strong and in control of my life! I have no excuse to complain anymore, because the only person controlling me is myself. This life principle is written within Alcoholics Anonymous Serenity Prayer: "God, grant me the serenity to accept the things I cannot change, the courage to change the things I can, and the wisdom to know the difference."

I can't count how many times throughout my life I have asked myself, what is the purpose of living? Why am I here? What am I supposed to be doing with my life? Does my life have any meaning? These are all valid questions, and they are also deeply philosophical and spiritual questions. Sometimes these questions go unanswered for a person's entire life. I know that this can be extremely frustrating and debilitating. Often, people just cruise through life, and not even think of questions like this.

To live a life without purpose is like walking through life in a cloud of mist, feeling lost and bewildered. This lack of direction often leads to a lack of motivation and generates a sense of hopelessness. It is like there is this huge ocean of potential within us, yet we are too blind, scared, stubborn, hurt, proud, loud, controlled, big, or small to look for it and discover what it is. It is only in the sacred space within us that our chattering mind stops, and allows our wisdom to speak to us. It is during this time that we can discover who we really are and why we are here. But to hear it, we must listen deeply. That is where you will find the joy within.

Our life purpose is more than living and/or suffering. It is also so much more than survival, or working from nine to five to pay the bills. It is more than meeting our basic needs; what I have discovered is that it is about meeting our intrinsic needs. By intrinsic, I mean our instinctual, innate, divine sense of what we know we have to do with our God-given gifts. It is like, when we were born, we came into this world, as a clean slate, waiting to be influenced and shaped by our families, friends, society, and our life experiences. All these things combined carve out our life purpose, which is just awaiting our discovery.

Despite our differences, every one of us has a burning desire and an inner knowing of what we have come here to do. It has been there the whole time, waiting for you and me to find it; it has been whispering in your heart and mind since the moment you were born. The key to its discovery is your ability to overcome the challenges that life puts across your path. You must rise above these barriers to find your talents, passion, and life purpose. Once you have worked out what your life purpose is, you then need to allow it to drive your life, instead of being mesmerised by things, like a moth to the light, that take you in the wrong direction, down the wrong path.

Finding your life purpose is like finding the most precious gift in the world. Every single one of us has a set of wonderful skills that we were either born with, or have learnt or experienced. It is a divine gift. Yet so many of us simply choose to ignore the silent murmurs of our mind, body, and spirit. Despite, life constantly trying to point us in the right direction, often we are just so self-centred and ego-driven that we either don't want to hear what our calling is, or we are too busy trying to distract or numb ourselves, and make ourselves happy by getting stuff, that we miss the true meaning and purpose of life.

Working out what your purpose in life is takes determination and persistence. When I first started wanting to know what my purpose was, I had nowhere near enough life experience to be able to work out what it was. I did know what I valued in life, and what skills, talents, and knowledge I already had, but the missing ingredient was passion. I had to work out, no matter what happens tomorrow, what I will always think is important, and what I will always want to focus on and do, even if I don't get paid to do it. When you can answer these questions, you will be on the right track to finding your purpose. What makes you tick? What makes you lose track of time? What makes you laugh and smile? What makes you feel good? That's your purpose.

When I couldn't pinpoint my purpose, I realised that the things I had not taken into consideration were the things that I wasn't so good at. It turned out that these were things that I had thought I'd failed at, things that annoyed me to the core, and things that I felt were unjust. These were experiences that I had wanted to bury and pretend did not happen. I wanted to forget them, hide from them, and not acknowledge that I had learnt anything from them. I learnt that this is exactly what I should not be ignoring, because it was these life experiences that I'd had that were also trying to help me discover what my purpose in life was.

When I shifted my thinking to include both the good and not-so-good experiences, skills, talents, lessons, and passions in my life, this helped me discover my true life purpose.

The final thing that helped me understand what my purpose in life was about was reading a book called "The Purpose Driven Life" by Rick Warren. Everything that I needed from this book was in its opening words. The message was as clear as a bell!

"It's not about you!"

Those words spoke directly to my heart. All these years, I had been searching for the answer to my question, "Who am I?" I was ashamed to admit that, during that whole time, not for one minute did I worry about the growth of another soul. All I had focused on was me! How shameful! When I had this insight, it was such a valuable lesson to me that I just knew I had to share it. When I realised that, all this time, the purpose of my life was to help others, this is when I knew exactly what I had been born to do. I knew in that moment that this is what we have all come to this Earth to do. I remember hearing in a YouTube clip about someone's near-death experience, that during a life review, when they got to heaven, one of God's questions was, "What did you do with the life that you have been given?" Now, if we knew that we were going to be asked this question the minute that we got to heaven, then perhaps we would be more determined to work out what our purpose is while we are still on Earth, and fulfil it. Having the answer to this question will help you know if you've found your purpose in this life, or if you are still looking. If you can't think of anything special, significant, or meaningful that you've done throughout your life thus far, then perhaps it's indicating that you're not on task, on track, or on purpose. Which means that God, the Universe, or Ancestors have been unable to use the skills you've been bestowed with to help others through you. Once I understood that these gifts and talents, challenges, and experiences that I, and you, have been blessed with are to be used for a specific purpose, and that the purpose is often not clear to us at the time, but once you know, you know.

With this new knowledge, I now breeze through the day, and let myself be guided by my passion for healing. I now realise that it is through helping others that my purpose in life is always more than fulfilled, and equally blessed.

After discovering your life purpose, you might start wondering: what about life values? Are these inbuilt from the moment that we are born? Life's values are like a moral compass that points us in the right direction. Certain values might be more appealing to you than others, and often they stem from our parents, carers, extended families, and the society in which we live.

All societies have been guided by an array of values that determine what is right and wrong. There are hundreds of values, but the one thing in common is that they are all a positive nature. Without any sense of values, anarchy would reign. In other words, this world of ours would be in a mess, with no rules or regulations, no right or wrong, no discipline or consequences, and no value for life or anything within its realm. Pretty scary concept! If values mean having respect, compassion, love, wisdom, honesty, passion, and hope, then please count me in.

Everyone's values in life will be slightly different, and that is the beauty of free will, and the beauty of being human. Values help us to figure out if our lives are in balance, and if we are living our lives by our most important values. These values, without doubt, go hand in hand with our life's purpose. Often, when we think about values, we consider questions like: "Am I happy?" "Am I using my time wisely?" "Do I feel alright?" "Do I love what I am doing?" "Does my life have meaning?"

In the past, I would have said if you can answer "yes" to these questions, then you are living a purpose- and value-driven life. Now that I have come to realise that life is not about me, it has helped to take the focus off "me", "my", and "I". It has made me realise that my life is about service to others. As soon as I took the three little words "me", "my", and "I" out of the equation, I was able to easily find my true purpose. In doing this, I easily remembered what I valued in life, and more importantly, how I could best help others to become the best version of themselves, if they wanted that help.

Along the way to finding our purpose, based on our values, we often need to set goals. Whenever I talk about goals, I am always drawn to the analogy of a game of sport. Imagine that you are playing a game of football, soccer, netball, or basketball. There are always two teams, and there are always two set of goals, one at either end of the court or field. By having a set of goals, we can decide who wins the game, and who needs to improve their skills, or who need to put in more effort to win. I'm sure you would all agree: what is the point of playing the game if there are no goals? When we remember to apply this to the game of life, we can quickly see the purpose of having goals in our lives. When you think about it, do you even have any goals that you are using to guide you through your life? Often, we just go from day to day without any goals. So how do we even know how we are progressing in life? What you will find, if you do not have any goals and nothing to aim for in life, is that you travel aimlessly through life. As they say, nothing lost, nothing gained. This is when life becomes meaningless. There is the famous quote from "Alice in Wonderland" that nicely captures having no goals, direction, or purpose in life. "Alice said, 'Would you tell me, please, which way I ought to go from here?' The Cheshire

Cat said, 'That depends a good deal on where you want to get to.'"

I bet you spend more time planning a holiday or a birthday party than planning your life and setting goals for your future. I know this because I too am guilty of this. If we aren't natural planners or goal-setters, what pushes us to strive for anything in our life? We are all given a perfectly opportune time at the end of one year, and the beginning of the next. That's right — Happy New Year. We are all enthusiastic at this time of the year; we make New Year's resolutions, and we are full of determination. Usually, this is just momentary, and lasts for two weeks, or if you're lucky, about two months.

Tell me, if you don't make the change at the turn of the year, when do you set yourself a new goal? What pushes you to the limit, to say, "Enough is enough?" Usually, it's when push comes to shove, "when the wheels fall off", and when life's challenges force you to do something you wouldn't normally do. Often, it takes a crisis before we get the message that things only change if things change. Even though growth is important for us as individuals, I want to encourage you to jump before you are pushed. Don't wait for a crisis before you decide that it's time to change. Take control of your life, and make the decision that will bring about the change that you need and want. Set those goals, and just take one little step at a time.

Ask yourself the question, where do I want to be in life by thirty years, twenty years, ten years, five years, one year's time, six months, one month, two weeks, one week, tomorrow, today, and right now? Then you can work your way back up the happiness scale, and find the easiest way to achieve your goals. You also have the advantage of knowing what it is that you need to do, strive for, and achieve at each step of the way. You can have a thirty-year plan, which is made up of a whole lot of smaller goals; these will add up to your purpose in life, based on all your life values.

Now, before your thirty years plus is up, I'm sure that there are a least one hundred things you want to do, and not enough time to do them all. This is when we all need a "Bucket List." The term "Bucket List" is an expression that lists the things that you want to do before you die. My "Bucket List" is based on all the life principles about which I have just talked. Life purpose, life values, and goals in life. These principles are all similar and related to each other, and I am guided by each of them, and they help to steer me in my everyday decision-making. It does not mean that my life is predictable; it just means that I consciously choose the direction that my life is taking.

It truly helps to know my life purpose, values, and goals. They remind me who I am, and what I am here for. My goals give me a zest for life, and keep me on purpose and well-balanced. It does not mean that life has become completely smooth sailing; it just means that, when I get blown off course, it's much easier for me to get back on track.

Once I discovered my purpose in life, my focus changed to asking myself again what the purpose of life is. To answer that question, I had to do some more deep diving, soul-searching, and personal research. When I looked inside myself, I felt like my soul told me that the purpose of life was to overcome pain and suffering, to learn to turn the other cheek, to learn to be the best version of myself, and to help others. When I think about the typical answers people always give, they would be to be happy, to grow, and to love others. People who are on their deathbeds say the meaning of life is about fulfilling your dreams, about spending quality time with loved ones, about expressing your feelings, nurturing friendships, choosing to be happy, and about facing our fears.

Children believe that life is about taking risks, playing, learning, and loving others. People who have had near-death experiences believe that the purpose of life is about creating the life that we want, to love, and to forgive. Spiritual gurus believe that the purpose of life is to raise our awareness, consciousness, and vibration by changing our thoughts, reflecting on learnings, gaining wisdom, and working towards "enlightenment", and overall loving one another. Hindus believe that we are born in debt to the Gods, and therefore need to right those wrongs by doing virtuous deeds through good moral and ethical tasks, thereby balancing karma and resulting in an enjoyable life. The Dalai Lama, the spiritual head of Tibetan Buddhism, believes that the meaning of life is one of understanding suffering, which we can end through meditation, spiritual and physical dedication, good behaviour, or karma. This will help us achieve inner peace and happiness, and move towards enlightenment. Jesus taught us that we should love one another as we love ourselves. He also said we should replace hate with love, and anger with kindness, which brings us peace. We should treat others the way we want to be treated. Jesus wanted us to have faith, and pray to God, to express our gratitude. We need not ask for things, for they have already been given to us by the grace of God. The biggest thing Jesus wanted us to practice was forgiveness, and promised that it would bring peace into our own lives. Mother Teresa simply wanted us to be of service to others, and to love one another, and to give wholehearted, free service to the poorest of the poor.

The one common word that keeps appearing in the above teachings about the meaning of life is "love". I know that it may sound simplistic, and even naïve, but sometimes we make everything so complex that we lose touch with the true meaning of life. If we know that life is about love, then it would seem obvious that the one thing that stops us from loving each other is often our unwillingness to forgive one another. "The Bible" reminds us in the "Lord's Prayer", in Matthew 6: 9-13", "And forgive us our trespasses, as we forgive those who trespass against us."

Yet despite this knowledge, often our ego thinks that it knows best, and that we are not in the wrong, and we shouldn't have to apologise— it's the other person's fault. Our ego decides that we should punish the other person for their wrongdoings. We stubbornly dig our heels in, and we think revengeful and hurtful thoughts about others. We withdraw our love. All the time, we are hoping that this will hurt them more than we are hurting. So, tell me this: Who do you think you are really hurting? That's right, in the end, it's you, and it doesn't involve anyone else.

The day before I wrote this chapter, I learnt something important about forgiveness. I was shown a very practical answer to a remarkably simple principle. It helped me to clearly understand my own shortcomings in forgiveness, and was a gentle reminder that I need to continually work on this principle. When I went to work, I had a backpack on my back. Generally, it is empty and only has a few things in it, like my lunch, a drink bottle, and phone, but this one morning I knew that I wanted to work on the topic in my book about unconditional love and forgiveness, so I went through my bookcase at home and found all the books that I remembered reading about forgiveness, and loaded them into my backpack. I had ten heavy books that were full of years of wisdom and knowledge, which I would need to help pull together my own thoughts and knowledge around this principle. I was now all set to head off to work. First, I lugged the backpack into my car. When I got to town, I knew that I would need to walk for twenty minutes to get to my workplace. I heaved my loaded backpack onto my back, and trudged to work. By the time I got to work, my shoulders were aching, my feet were sore, and my back was hurting. Despite this, I swung into action, did the usual checking of emails, and went to my scheduled meeting.

After a brief conversation during a meeting, I quickly realised that my blood was starting to boil, and I was beginning to feel an angry dragon raise its ugly head deep inside my heart. After my first feelings of anger and resentment, my mind went straight into "negative overdrive." After I left the meeting, I spent far too long churning the scenario over and over in my mind, thinking about how I could have changed the outcome. I finally decided that there wasn't anything I could do to change the situation, so I began plotting what I could do to "get even" with this person.

It is clear now that all this thinking was focussed on the past, and that any thoughts towards the future were not of a positive nature either. By the end of the day, I was feeling very tired, very grumpy, and beaten. The last thing that I wanted to do was lug my heavy bag full of forgiveness books back to the car! Despite not feeling motivated at all, I knew it had to be done, so off I set. It wasn't until I nearly reached my car, with my aching shoulders, sore feet, and painful back, that a thought struck me like a bolt of lightning. I suddenly realised that, due to all the other demands of the day, I didn't even get a chance to pull out any of the books on forgiveness. It then dawned on me that, of all the days that I needed that wisdom and knowledge of forgiveness, this most certainly was one of them. Yet despite having everything right at my fingertips, or in my backpack, I chose to ignore the lessons on forgiveness that were there to be learnt. I put myself through relentless, unnecessary physical, emotional, mental, and spiritual pain and torture, just because I was too stubborn to be the bigger person and forgive the other person.

The question that dawned on me because of this experience was: how many times have we all trudged through life, knowing what the most logical, wise, and right choice would be, yet being too determined about being angry and being right to do anything about it? To save yourself pain, time, and heartache, it's wise to get that emotional baggage off your back. Healing requires forgiveness, which starts with the word "sorry". I know it's hard to admit you were in the wrong, and it can be confronting, but it's not impossible, and the benefits outweigh the risks of losing face.

Once we have understood the concept of unconditional love and forgiveness, it is then that we can truly let go of the past, and move freely into the future. It has only been in recent years that I have been able to personally do this. To achieve this, I had to take responsibility for my actions during the breakdown of my marriage, which empowered me to look back at that period of my life and no longer feel a sense of guilt, bitterness, resentment, anger, sadness, hurt, and pain.

It took me about five years of beating myself up, and holding on to those angry, hurt-filled, guilt-ridden feelings, before I realised that enough was enough and I decided to "let go" of the past. I knew that my connection to the past was affecting my present and future life. When I realised that the key to moving forward in my life could only happen once I had forgiven others, I immediately understood that I had to forgive myself, and I also needed to forgive my ex-husband, Rusty. If I had not done this, I would still be living in the past, and I would not have learnt a thing from that experience, and I certainly could not be fully present in any present moment. The hardest part was to make that decision to "let go" of the past, and ultimately "let go" of him and our shared memories.

I knew that it was the last bit of invisible thread that I was holding onto, that connected me to my past. I had to cut the ties between him and me, and me and him.

In hundreds of self-help books that I have read, they all state that forgiveness is the absolute key to healing. I knew that I had to do a forgiveness exercise, which I have adapted from world-renowned author Louise Hay's book — "You Can Heal Your Life."

To start off with, I sat quietly and focused on the person I wanted to forgive.

I then said aloud, the following:

I _______________, forgive you _______________ for _______________.

I wish you had _______________, but you didn't, and I now set you free. Thank you!

I did the above exercise for all the past feelings of hurt, resentment, guilt, and anger that I could remember. It took a long time to get through the list, and yes, it was an extensive list and an exhausting task. At the end of it, I had to do the same for myself, and forgive myself for the hurtful things that I had also done in the relationship. I felt lighter, like a weight had lifted from my shoulders. I felt free!

Two weeks after I had done this exercise, I was then ready to phone my ex-husband and let him know that I was sorry for the past pain that I had caused him. I understand not everyone can do this. By the end of the brief conversation, I know that we each felt a deep sense of relief. The past pain, hurt, and guilt dissolved, left my body, and set me free. The attachment to my past had been "let go". It was a very releasing experience, and one that I recommend you try.

Now no matter how much I think I know, I also know that there is someone who has discovered a new way of doing things that is better than what I've tried in the past. This is also the case with forgiveness. I came across a book called "Radical Forgiveness", which was written by Colin Tipping, rest his soul. It is an absolute must-read. It completely tips every other forgiveness theory on its head. By doing the provided worksheets, it gives you the opportunity to take a deeper look at the situation in which you have felt hurt, and completely helps you to unpack the situation and see it from a different perspective, possibly one that you may not have previously been willing or able to see. I promise you that "Radical Forgiveness" is worth every cent, and it will give you peace of mind at once. Now that is priceless.

Just as this "Radical Forgiveness" book came to me at the exact right moment in time, so did my concept and understanding of the law of attraction. I have always wondered what it was all about, and I had always wanted to be able to unlock its secret. Have you ever felt that magnetic attraction you have when Prince Charming walks into the crowed room, and your eyes interlock, and there is just this overwhelming sense of attraction? Maybe that is your experience of the law of attraction, but that isn't exactly my understanding of what the law of attraction is all about. What I am talking about is a universal law that is as relevant as the "law of gravity", which ensures that things always fall downwards towards the centre of the Earth. The law of attraction ensures that like attracts like. I know that this is starting to sound scientific, and I am no scientist, so I will start with what I do know, and try to make it simple.

Everything in this world is made of energy. Energy is something that we know is there, but we can't necessarily see it, which is like electricity. We know it exists because we see appliances operating because of it, yet electricity itself we cannot physically see. We can see the aftermath of the damage that lightning, which is a giant spark of electricity, does if it strikes a tree. We also know that, if we accidentally experience an electric shock we can painfully feel it, and it can be lethal. One way that we can almost see, or feel, the pull of energy is through the pull of two magnets. Magnets have a north, negative, and a south, positive, pole; these opposite poles attract each other, but the same poles repel, or push, each other away. The strength of the magnetic energy, or field, is dependent on whether you work with the energy or against it. The law of attraction, which we can't see or feel, works similarly to that of a magnet.

The law of attraction is the pull, or attraction, that occurs between your mind and what you want, or don't want, to physically manifest. "What you think about the most is what you attract into your life." Buddha explains it simply by saying, "All that you are is a result of what you think about the most." If you think about the implications of that statement, then it certainly does explain why you are where you are in your life, no matter where that may be. In other words, your mind attracts anything that you think about, and it can't tell the difference between whether your thoughts are good, bad, positive, or negative … it simply attracts. You might be thinking that this all sounds great, but, "How does that affect me?" Now, it's important to realise that this law works whether you want it to work or not. There is no on or off switch. It just is! Now, if you can't stop it from working, then you may as well work with it. The more aware of your own thinking that you become, the easier it is to control what you attract. This is called being "mindful". And, like a magnet, if you think negative thoughts, you will attract negative experiences, and if you think positive thoughts, you will attract positive experiences.

I hear you asking, "How do I make it work for me?" When you think about it, it just seems too simple, and if it's so simple to achieve, then why aren't we all rich and leading happy, fulfilling, wonderful, prosperous lives? The answer is that we don't all think the same consistent positive thoughts. Everyone secretly has a victim mentality, and we think that we have lived a worse life than the person next to us. Hence, most people believe that, because of their circumstances, the world really does owe them. The nature of those thoughts is obviously negative, so if the law attracts what you think about the most, then you are just going to continue to attract more of the same negative outcomes. Unless you become aware of your negative thoughts, and change them into positive thoughts or vibrations, then you can sadly be promised a not-so-happy life.

The law of attraction has secret principles, which are universal laws. We have already accepted that everything is energy, and this energy constantly vibrates. These levels, or rates, of vibrations are influenced by the nature of your thoughts, and you can energetically attract things to yourself, or repel things from yourself, simply through positive or negative thinking. The happier and more positive the thoughts, the stronger and higher the vibration. The sadder and more negative the thoughts, the lower and slower the vibration, and the weaker the attraction. If you'd like to learn about the emotional scale, which is described in depth in best-selling book "Ask and It Is Given" by Ester Hicks, it really helps you understand how to lift yourself from a lower vibration into a higher vibration, and hence vastly improve your ability to manifest easily by simply reaching for a better-feeling thought. Stronger passion and beliefs generate a feeling of already having what you want, and the more positive the thoughts, the higher, or faster, the energy vibrates, therefore the faster the physical manifestation. The main point here is, as W. Clement Stone, who was mentored by the author of "Think and Grow Rich" — Napoleon Hill — lived by the quote, "whatever the mind can conceive, it can achieve." William Stone was a real rags-to-riches story. He authored a book called "The Success System That Never Fails." It outlined that you must use your mind to create, visualise, and attract what you want, need, and believe in. It might seem simplistic; however, the more that you want something, the more likely it is to materialise, because it is vibrating at the same rate as your desire. Please note that desire alone does not bring about the things you want. To want something just means that you really want it. It doesn't mean that you can see yourself with it; it just means that you want it. You also must have faith that it will come to fruition. To have faith means that you go beyond desire, and beyond the logical thinking mind. This is when our feelings come into action. Our feelings are what impact our vibrational frequency and attraction. When we feel and experience emotions like love, joy, peace, happiness, forgiveness, and gratitude, this makes it easier for the Universe, our Ancestors, to deliver what we truly desire, imagine, and ask for. Because our thoughts are vibrating at a very high rate. So, without question, you just need to believe in your heart of hearts, have unwavering faith, and see and feel yourself having it in your mind's eye. This is what having faith is. It's imagining that you have already achieved, or got, what you have vividly dreamed about. You've visualised, imagined, and most importantly, felt yourself already having it. This is when it's a done deal! When you consistently marry your positive thoughts with high-vibrational, positive feelings, that is when the magic of physical manifestation happens. The better you get at controlling, or mastering, your thoughts and feelings, the quicker physical manifestation happens and your reality shifts. Some people refer to this as heart-mind coherence. Basically, when your thoughts in your mind and your feelings in your heart, are in tune with each other, and are totally balanced, they create a very clear and focused energy — a high-vibrational signal that draws and aligns experiences and opportunities to you, to help you achieve your envisioned dreams. This shifts your physical reality.

I know that if you are like many non-believers, then you are stuck on the "how" — how are we going to achieve this? Worrying about the how does not show the Universe, our Ancestors, that you have complete faith that your thoughts will become your reality. What you are really telling the Universe, our Ancestors, is that you don't have faith in its ability to deliver. In fact, you are telling the Universe, our Ancestors, that you will put a backup plan in place, just in case it doesn't really work. This then becomes a negative affirmation, instantly lowering your vibrational state by allowing feelings of doubt, fear, depression, sadness, and hopelessness to creep in, making you question your faith and beliefs; hence "what you don't believe you also achieve." When we have a negative thought, it makes us feel negative, and then that's what we begin to believe, instantly lowering the law of attraction vibration. This is destined to attract the worst outcome, not the best. This then becomes your new reality. This is when you clench your fists, stomp your foot, and say, "See, I told you none of that law of attraction mumbo jumbo works." It really is about getting the right balance. It's about deciding what you want, consistently choosing it and sticking to the decision, being happy with your decision, and being open to suggestions and signs about necessary actions that you need to take to clear the path, allowing your manifested desire to materialise. This may be in the form of impulses, ideas, following hunches, and being receptive to all things good. This is when we become "inspired", which is like a derivative of "in spirit". It's allowing the energy forces to move through you, and push you out of your comfort zone, to help attract what you desire. It's not about "making" it happen, but allowing it to happen. Continually having faith and a sense of gratitude makes space for this desire to appear in your life. Keeping your emotions consistently at a high-vibrational frequency will guarantee its materialisation. Doing what you love, and loving what you do. Realising that you deserve, and already have, everything your heart has ever desired. It's a universal law that is undeniable. So, become a magnet to your own dreams, and turn them into the new reality that you've dreamed about.

This poem captures the "law of attraction" principles perfectly.

You Can If You Think You Can!

If you think you are beaten, you are,

if you think you dare not, you don't.

If you like to win, but you think you can't,

It is almost certain you won't.

If you think you'll lose, you're lost,

For out in the world we find,

Success begins with a fellow's will.

It's all in the state of mind.

If you think you are outclassed, you are,

You've got to think high to rise,

You've got to be sure of yourself before

You can ever win a prize.

Life's battles don't always go

To the stronger or faster man.

But soon or late the man who wins,

Is the man who thinks he can.

-C. W. Longenecker-

What C.W. Longenecker, and so many other inspirational leaders before him, have discovered is that you are the only one that creates your reality. You are here to create the world around you that you choose. This is one of the main purposes of living. It is for us to learn to harness the incredible source of energy that we all have equal access. This energy has no limits and no restrictions. It does not discriminate. It only recognises positive and negative thinking. The only restrictions in place are those that we place upon ourselves through our unconscious and uncontrolled thoughts. Life is completely abundant, and the Universe, our Ancestors, absolutely have an endless supply of everything that everyone has ever needed or imagined. It's just a matter of believing, and feeling it into existence. And what you will find is the joy within.

Chapter 14
Beyond Identity

As a little girl, we used to visit an aunty and uncle who lived in a country town in New South Wales. The backdrop to their house was a huge mountain. At the age of five, it seemed gigantic to me. I remember holding my uncle's hand, and we would set off on an adventure to climb that mountain together. On reflection, it now seems like a symbolic depiction of my life's journey.

People think of life as a mountain that must be conquered, and it's supposed to be hard and arduous, and you're supposed to struggle, stumble, and sometimes even fall. You're supposed to feel like quitting and turning back, and you're supposed to get hurt along the way. You're supposed to travel this journey all on your own, just to prove that you can do it by yourself. You're supposed to lose your way because no one gave you a map with instructions on how to navigate through life. Somehow, you instinctively know that you're supposed to be heading in an upward direction towards the top, because you just feel as though that is where the meaning of life will be revealed.

If this is the case, how do we know how far along our journey on the mountain of life we are? Do we ever stop to take stock of our life and think, "Am I still on track?" "How am I travelling?" "Have I progressed any further up the mountain?" "Do I even want to climb this mountain?" "Is there really going to be something at the top of this mountain?" "Who even says there is a peak?" "When will I know that I have arrived?" "When I get there, who or what will I find?" "Is it really worth it?"

I have learnt the answers to those questions, sometimes with the help of others, but often from life itself. Often, when you personally learn the lesson, the experience has more meaning. You feel as though you have earned the knowledge. It wasn't just given to you on a silver platter; you worked hard to achieve it, and you have the emotional scars, or stripes, to prove it.

What I've come to realise is that the peak of the mountain is like a metaphor for your discovery of consciousness. It is the journey that we take through life, always seeking answers. At every intersection, crossroads, or challenge that we encounter in life, we are given a choice to rise above it, or to become stagnated and suffer a bit, or a whole lot more, before finally deciding that enough is enough. Finally recognising that it's time to move through and beyond our perceived pain. Everyone is climbing at a different rate; everyone's level of experience or understanding is different, and everyone's capability to cope with the rubble or trouble along the way is varied. Everyone's levels of strength ebbs and flows, depending on what you've encountered before and after each catastrophe. However, usually after each challenging moment, our level of awakening slightly increases. We learn lessons, we grow, and we often remember not to fall down that hole again. It's like a light is momentarily turned on within us, reminding us of who we really are. It gives us a glimpse of hope, a drop of happiness, and a promise of finding true love of life and of ourselves.

I recently learnt that life has deceived us all. We all think that we are here to achieve happiness, but when you think deeply about it, do you honestly know any people who are truly and completely happy with their life and with themselves? Do you know anyone who doesn't experience challenges in their life? Do you know anyone who has seriously tried to climb the mountain of life, successfully reached the top, knows all the answers, and wants to help you and others to get there too? I can guarantee that there are very few people who can honestly claim to have achieved this. What you will find is that those who have found this inner sense of peace or enlightenment are not standing on top of the mountain shouting out life's answers to the world. The wise ones say little, despite knowing that they know everything and nothing. All I know is that I've had a glimpse of it, and I describe it as finding the joy within. That is why I've wanted to share my insight with you, in the hope that this book is a bit of a guide to help you along your life's journey.

I have discovered that there are countless theories outlining the various developmental themes, or stages in life, that we go through. All these theories name or label our patterns of behaviour, and help us understand the path that we have chosen. Often, we spend years and thousands of dollars going to a counsellor, psychologist, therapist, or life coach to discover the answers to our perceived life's dilemmas. The thing that I have found from my search for my identity is that "we already have the answers within ourselves." I have wanted to know "Who am I?" since my teenage years, and it has taken fifty-plus years and immeasurable personal growth to get to this point. The writing of this book has helped me to discover "Who am I?" and to find the joy within. This book was not written overnight; it has taken me twenty-eight years to write. Just under half of my life on Earth. Seeing that figure written on these pages is shocking to me. When I started writing this book, it was a response to my postpartum psychosis. I wanted to unjumble my chaotic thoughts. I wanted to unravel my past, sort out my emotions, and lay it all out on pages, so I could make sense of my inner world, which, during that time, made no sense whatsoever. What I had no idea about was how long that process was going to take. How many more lessons in life I'd have to learn. How many more challenging moments I'd have to experience, overcome, evaluate, and process. How many more days and nights of self-induced suffering I'd have to endure. How many more tears would I have to shed? The list seemed endless, and achieving the goal was like chasing the end of a rainbow.

I never suspected that I could have worked this out for myself. All my life, I have been able to find every answer I ever wanted in a book. As you can imagine, it came, as a bit of a shock when, after searching for the answer through books, I was still none the wiser. It took fifty-plus years to work out that I simply needed to look within myself, instead of searching for the answers outside of myself. When I finally worked this out for myself, the only thing left to do was simply laugh. Even after saying this, I think of a laughing Buddha that sits by people's front door for prosperity. I now know why he is laughing, and it's simply because "he knows." What he knows is information that is deep within our souls. It is the answer to all the questions we have about life; he understands the meaning of life. He sees what a mess we unnecessarily make of our lives, so instead of being angry and depressed, why not just laugh? Be grateful for what we have, and stop worrying about what we don't have. It will come — especially if you laugh a lot.

So, after fifty years of searching for my identity, I have finally come to be at peace with myself. What I now know is that I was nowhere near ready to accept this information when I first started searching, and I had to go through everything that I went through before I could truly appreciate this new understanding. What I've realised is that we are all on a journey that we must go through. No one is immune to this journey. It is like a rite of passage. It's part of our humanness. It is part of our experience. Despite wanting to rescue others, that's not up to us to do either. They need to experience their own sorrows and struggles to help them appreciate the beauty of life when it comes, not only as a lesson, but a blessing.

I genuinely believed, when I was thirty years old, that I needed to look deeply into the past to work out who I was, what I was here to do, and ultimately find my identity. I thought this would also give me an idea about why I was here and what the point of my life was. I thought that this meant learning all that I could about my Aboriginal ancestry, and finding out all that I could about my birth mum, my brothers and sisters, and extended Aboriginal family. I thought that it meant I needed to take my cultural spirit back "home" to Country and reconnect with my land. I thought it meant I had to learn all that I could about my Aboriginal culture and our shared black history. I thought that I needed to understand the impacts of colonisation, how that had affected my Aboriginal family, and how that had created a legacy of intergenerational trauma that was continuously being handed down from one generation to the next. So, over the next twenty years I did that informal, action-based research. I had reunions with my birth family, I travelled back to my traditional Kamilaroi Country, and studied and read all that I could at university about Aboriginal culture and history. I chose jobs within the Aboriginal education and health sector. I attended every conference that had an Aboriginal content focus. I took every opportunity to research births, deaths, and marriage records, to connect the dots and try to piece together our family's story. In my search for my identity, I learnt that my mother, Joan Margaret West, had lived a hard life. She became a young mum at the age of eighteen, she started to bring up our eldest brother, Wayne, with the help of her mother and father, Nana Terrisa and Grandfather Bindi, while living on an Aboriginal Mission in Brewarrina, during the reign of the Assimilation Policy. It wasn't until I was forty-seven years old that, for the first time in my life, I discovered a forty-second film clip that was recorded in 1958, where I saw Mum walking and holding our second eldest brother, David, on her hip. I had only ever seen one photograph of my mum, which was taken not long before she died in 1981. The photo of this Aboriginal woman, standing there looking straight into the camera, looked worn out and beaten by life. That woman, my mum, was vastly different to the young, vibrant, strong woman I saw in the short video clip, walking with a baby on her hip. In that moment, I realised all the lies that the Department of Children's Services had led me to believe. I remembered all the lies written as cold, hard facts and "supposed truth", written in permanent ink, in every document and record I'd ever accessed. In that moment of seeing my mum walking so gracefully and confidently with our brother on her hip I learnt so much about who she was as a young, proud, strong, fun-loving, kind, caring, humble, timid, Aboriginal woman, full of life, hopes and dreams. This clip gave me a gift that all the paperwork and reading in the world could never have given me. It put a personality to a name, and gave me back a large part of my own identity, of who I was and where I'd come from. It unwittingly captured the long line of tradition, culture, and strength in our Aboriginal family's history and identity. It silently spoke to my heart, telling me where I came from, who I belonged to, where I was connected, and how I fit in. It really was what I thought I had been looking for on my journey of life. It felt like the answers I'd been seeking had been provided in just forty seconds. It brought me a sense of peace that I'd been seeking my whole life.

This knowledge, plus a whole lot of other family history research that my sister's daughter had been discovering, has helped to fill in the gaps in my knowledge about my Aboriginal family, but mostly the gaps in what happened to that strong lady, my mum. This clip and photograph filled in so many blanks about my mum — the woman who I saw walk with such pride in 1958, right through to the older, worn-out looking Aboriginal woman who stood leaning, defeated, against an old Holden station wagon in 1981. From what I can tell, my mum had my brother Wayne in 1957, and didn't have any more children for another five years. My mum and her then partner were hard workers, and worked a fencing job to try and make ends meet. The records showed that my mum and her partner were falsely accused of stealing fencing wire. As a result, they were charged and locked up in custody. Wayne, my eldest brother was removed from Mum's care and placed in Kinchela Boys Home, and hence the slippery slope with child protection began from 1962. For the next ten years, Mum was almost pregnant every year, with the youngest of her children, the triplets, being born in 1976. In 1964, Mum lost both of her parents within three months of each other. I can barely imagine the pain and the overwhelming amount of grief and loss my mum had to cope with. Mum's mental health severely suffered during this time, which added fuel to the child removal justification. Not only did Mum have a schizophrenia diagnosis and many hospital admissions over the years, but she also turned to alcohol and experienced many unhealthy relationships in the search for love, while trying to dull the overwhelming sense of unresolved grief, loss, and pain. Mum had repeatedly lost all rights to see her children, and had lost her brother and both of her parents, who were the sole support people who helped her cope with the struggles of life.

Over the years, Mum had about six different partners. None of them were healthy relationships. The last relationship being the most toxic, and he was the person who tragically ended my mum's life through alcohol-driven violence. It still shocks me to this day that this man walks freely in this country and served a minimal sentence for such a horrific crime against an Aboriginal woman — my mum.

Despite not figuring out the in-depth details of Mum's personal life history until later in my own life, I worked out that I similarly made at least two poor relationship choices. One would wonder how this could be, as I did not grow up with my birth mum and had never even saw her in her own toxic relationships. This is a mystery that we may never find the answers to, and it may be one of coincidence or subconscious choice that saw me follow a similar life pattern. But the one thing that I do know is that it is a pattern that I need to consciously break. Half the battle is achieved simply through my own awareness of the direction my mum's choices took her in, and the direction my own choices take me.

So, with all this new insight, I finally discovered more about my Aboriginality, which helped me momentarily feel fulfilled and whole. So why did I still feel as though I still wanted to know what my purpose in life was? What was the purpose of my story? Why was I here? Why did my mum, my siblings, and I have to go through this journey of separation, hurt, pain and suffering? I realised that there was no one that could answer those questions but myself. I had to go within myself to find the answers.

Thankfully, I did not have to go off to the Himalayan Mountains to find these answers. It took years of reflection and introspection to sift through all my experiences and finally discover who I am and what I'm here for. The answers came in waves when I sat quietly, or laid quietly in my bed at night, or at the beach, or under a tree, or in my rocking chair— or simply anywhere that I had a quiet moment to reflect. These moments of contemplation, or meditation, are known as "Dadirri", "Winanga-li", or "deep listening" to Aboriginal people. This is a term that Dr Miriam-Rose Ungunmerr Baumann has shared with the world. Dr Miriam-Rose describes it as the deep inner spring inside us — inner deep listening and quiet, still awareness. Dr Miriam-Rose said it is a gift that we all have within us. It's the only way to find the answers, about who we are, where we've been, and what we have come here to do or be. This is what I call "finding the joy within."

From looking, listening, and diving into the depths of my soul, I now know who I am, where I am from, and what my purpose in life is. I now remember who I am and realise that it is who I've always been and always will be — an eternal spirit, an ancestral being, infinite soul, divine being, universal soul. I am who I will be, even after I have left this physical world. I am light, I am soul, I am energy. I am one with all; I am part of the everlasting universal life force. I am pure love.

I now know that yes, I have a mind, but I am not my mind; yes, I have a body, but I am not my body; yes, I have a heart, but I am not my heart; yes, I have a soul, but I am not my soul. "I am" the eternal soul. As Dr Wayne Dyer puts it "I am that I am." "I am" whatever I choose to be. My body is just a physical vehicle that carries my spirit around on this earth for a brief time. My physical appearance, my Aboriginal culture, my Aboriginal family, my job, my story, my possessions, my qualifications and all the things that I thought make up who I am, are not who I am at all. They are all just props or a manuscript that have supported my individual and spiritual growth, role, ego and journey as a human on this Earth. Your props, circumstances, and characters on the life stage will be different to mine, but nonetheless complex. It's through our complexities and adversity that the light of awareness and growth is given the opportunity to shine through.

Before I started my journey to self-discovery, which I thought was finding out more about my Aboriginal identity— Who am I? — I thought all those worldly things made me who I was. I thought they shaped me into the person that I wanted to be, and I thought they would make me happy. I believed that these were all the pieces of my life puzzle that just needed to be put back together. It wasn't until I started truly looking at all of these "things" that I realised that's all they really are — just things! Labels, conditioning, a false identity that we identify with and tie ourselves to, believing it makes us who we are, measuring my importance, status, or success in life.

Life is not about things; life is about living in the moment, loving others, helping others, and being with others. I can have all the things I want in life, but if I can't share my joy, then life becomes worthless, pointless, and without purpose. If I can't be who I authentically am, then I am not being true to who I am. Life is abundant; it has everything that we need, because all we really need is love, and "I am" love. Love is energy. Love heals everything. When you begin to think about the things that you love in life, then you attract more love into your life, and the circle of life and energy continues to flow. This is when you get the most incredible physical manifestations possible.

I discovered that family is everything, and that to be loved without conditions and to give unconditional love is important beyond anything that money can buy. Everyone needs that sense of belonging, connection, and acceptance. Yet family doesn't have to be blood; family can be anyone who meets those essential and primal needs.

Most importantly, I discovered that the past only affects your future if you allow it. You are the author of your life, and you create your own reality. Every day is a new day with new opportunities. You can continue to look backwards to try to find something that you believe is missing, which you no longer have control over; you could imagine the future and dream of how things will be so amazing "if only"; or you can live in the present where we are no longer victims of the past or pining for a future that may never come. We can only ever be in the moment, and then it's gone. Life is an endless supply of moments. It is the whole point of living. But don't miss it, because in the blink of an eye it's gone.

Change is good; it is the only thing we can control in these moments. We can't change the past, and by blaming others, we give away our personal power and control. The only thing that we can really have control over, and change, is ourselves. How do we do this? With our thoughts. Life doesn't just happen to us; we are the experts and creators of our thoughts, and our thoughts are the vehicles that drive us into our future. Our travels will find us in a multitude of places and circumstances, but don't be surprised where you end up, because you are where you are because of the thoughts and choices you made. If you find yourself still getting angry, then maybe it's time to let go of that anger and give it to a higher source. The highest source of energy is love. It is the highest emotional vibration there is. Love helps you to forgive a past that you cannot change, let go, and move forward to embrace a future that brings self-acceptance and a true sense of inner peace. Letting go means giving up control over your life, but it also means having faith in something bigger than yourself. Forgiveness is the key to healing; it dissolves feelings of resentment, fear, anger, guilt, and hatred. It releases you from the past, as you are no longer trapped there by those negative thoughts, memories, or false stories. It makes room in your life for more love and reminds you to be grateful for what you do have, instead of focusing on what you don't have. Remember, every circumstance in life has a purpose, and you are part of life's bigger picture, or life's tapestry. You most certainly have a purpose in this life, and an unwavering sense of determination will help you find it. Never give up, and always be thankful for every experience, because every experience enriches your life. Whether it be a good or bad experience, is defined only by your own perspective.

I have discovered that, deep down "I" always knew who I was, and "I" was always happy with who "I" was. The true me, the pure light part of me that is deep within my soul, always knew the answers. The most exciting part is that you too can find the answers and joy within if you simply make the time to live in the moment, delve into the depths of your soul, and remember who you are, where you came from, why you are here, and where you will return to.

I hope that you thoroughly embrace this exact moment in your life and really absorb this insight about life, love, and who you really are! Time for a deep breath.

"Maslow's Hierarchy of Needs" talks about moving through various stages in life and reaching a pinnacle of "self-actualisation", which is a culmination of all that you have learnt and experienced in life — reaching your full potential and becoming the best that you can be. The theory states that, once you have achieved the basic safety needs in life, like having food, water, and shelter, then you feel safe, and you can work through finding love, family, and a sense of belonging to a community, which builds your self-esteem and self-respect. This is when your reputation and achievements in life are fulfilled, and you finally reach the "self-actualisation" stage, which is like reaching the top of the mountain. You've made it! It's like achieving the highest level of consciousness. It sounds easy, doesn't it! Yet life can be like a game of snakes and ladders. We move forward and we feel great, we hit some good luck, and it feels like we are really moving. Then we get a bit ungrateful and arrogant, forget the rules of life, and slip backwards down the snake. Sometimes further than we've ever been, and sometimes right back to the humble beginnings of the game. So, we reflect, ponder, and wonder what we did wrong. Sometimes we work it out for ourselves, but it's much quicker if we ask a higher power for some guidance and to put a bit of light on the subject. This game can go up and down like this for years and years. Some of us are quite unaware of the rules and just keep doing the same thing on a different day, which turns into months, years, and decades. Just like being on a merry-go-round. However, sometimes we get a hint, a hunch, a feeling that reminds us that if I do it this way, then I might have more luck. We test it! We seem amazed, so we try it again, and it works. Hallelujah, I must be doing something right. This is what we call insight! It's looking within and recognising, joining to dots, having an aha moment, putting the pieces of life's puzzle back together, and seeing the pattern. When you can do that, recognise that, and repeat that, this is when you've almost mastered the game of life. However, the wheels of life keep turning, and you need to keep your mental tools sharp. You must watch your inner thoughts like an eagle. When you can do this "without thinking", and there is not a shadow left in sight, this is "enlightenment." Your world will fill with light because there is not a place or space for darkness to hide. Light is pure love, or love is pure light. And it is deep within your soul, guiding you like a ship to its own shores at night. This is a place of pure joy!

All I ever dreamed about when I was a little girl was living happily ever after. I saw happiness in magazines and on television and read about it in fairy tales. So, I tried to follow suit. I grew up, got a good education, found a boyfriend, studied some more, got three qualifications that told me I was now smart and important, got married, bought a house, went on a honeymoon, travelled overseas, and had a baby. What I finally discovered, after achieving all of this, was that it still didn't make me happy. I was still lost. Still searching, still wondering, "Who am I?" Wondering, "What is my purpose in life?"

So, for me to achieve "self-actualisation", I originally went in search of my identity, trying to find out who I am based on my Aboriginal heritage and culture. What I eventually discovered was that I had to realise who I was not, before I could find out who I was. I had to lose the identity that I and the world had labelled me with. I had to become unattached from the human identity that defined me. I had to forget who the world wanted me to believe I'd become. I had to become unattached from everything that my ego wanted me to believe I deserved or earnt. I had to let go of a false past, and realise that, despite my life being full of success, achievements, and nice things, it wasn't who I really was, and it didn't make me happy. In fact, I had to lose myself before I could find myself. I had to let go of the past before I could move forward. I'd slipped down the snake, and now I had to work my way back up the ladder of life.

When I stopped my thoughts from identifying with the physical things of this world, all that I was left with was pure "love." Love is what we are. Love is energy vibrating at the highest frequencies. Love is what matter is made of. Love is the energy that drives us, binds us, surrounds us, and is everything in between. Love is all that matters. Love is where we've come from, and where we will return to. Ultimately, when I leave this physical world, all that I want to take with me are my happy memories, which are bathed in love and are love itself. This is why, when someone dies, it's hard for us to remember the bad things that they did, said, or made us feel. We idolise those who've left this Earth. We honour them and we grieve them, and we often forgive them once they're gone. This is because they have returned to pure source, and the shadows of their earthly life are left behind.

"Self-actualisation" or "enlightenment" is a worldwide concept. I have no doubt that this is also part of traditional Aboriginal culture. It just has many different language group words to describe it. Anthropologist Dr Bill Edwards who wrote the book titled "An Introduction to Aboriginal Societies" back in 1987, tried to capture this philosophical concept while living and working in the Anangu Pitjantjatjara Yankunytjatjara lands, and described it as "The Dreaming." It is cultural knowledge that has been handed down from ancestors through the generations, for thousands of years. Sometimes I used to think I have not been privileged with this cultural knowledge and had to learn about it from both university and "Universal" knowledge, which is available to every one of us. What I have discovered and interpreted as Universal knowledge, I believe, is my Ancestor's way of talking to me in this present moment, in my present circumstances, from deep inside myself. This provides me with a sense of peace, knowing who I am and where my

Ancestors came from. I am guided by an inner knowing of what's right and wrong, and aim to live my life within those sacred rules.

Whenever I am feeling unbalanced, this is when I know that I need to reconnect to the Source, my Ancestors, and ground myself through my culture. Go back to Country. Return to the land which we live, which sustains us. This is why Aboriginal people are so connected to the land, care for the land, and give thanks to the land for the gift of life it gives us. We recognise this daily. Without the land, we would all die. We treat the land like our own mother, who provides us with everything. This is why we "care for Country", because it cares for, nurtures, and sustains us. The land teaches us all these lessons that life also teaches us.

Dreaming songs, stories, dances, art, language, rituals, and lores are all ways that we communicate, and keep those lessons alive, and honour the spirit (energy) of the Country and land that we live on. Aboriginal culture is a living culture, kept vibrant through oral history. Much of the secret and sacred knowledge is passed on by Elders who have received the cultural right to that knowledge. This form of safe record-keeping protected future generations. It's what has kept us, as a culture of people, strong, safe, nurtured, and healthy in mind, body, and spirit for thousands and thousands of generations. It's the only thing that the white man has never been able to steal from us, right to this day. The land teaches us gratitude for every aspect of life. The wind, the rain, the fire, the sun, the plants, and the animals all nourish us and provide us with everything we need. When the land, our mother, gives to us, we need to give back to her. We acknowledge that every significant part of the landscape, such as a hill, rock, waterhole, tree, plains, lakes, billabong, creek, river, or other natural features, shows where our ancestral beings went before us. Acknowledging that is showing respect for where we have come from. I totally acknowledge how blessed I am that I live and walk in two worlds. I have drawn the best from both, and show gratitude daily for this privilege.

I know there would be thousands of "enlightened" people who have a deep understanding of life, but I believe that no matter how much self-exploration they, you or I do, there is always more to do. It is never-ending, and we will continue to learn until the day that we die and leave this physical earth realm.

Life is most definitely about the journey, and not the destination. I even question if there is a destination. Life is a cycle. Life-death-life. It is about living, growing, and dying. The minute that we stop growing, we start dying, and death is a new beginning. Our environment, and the plants and animals, demonstrate this daily. There is so much similarity between us and plants and animals, yet because of our egos, we believe we are separate and so much smarter than nature herself. You and I know how silly that sounds. We believe because we have a thinking brain, that we are smart. However, having a brain and being able to consciously use it, or being aware of how it is using us, are two distinctly different concepts. When you master this, the light turns on.

I have learnt that life is a combination of mountains and valleys, or snakes and ladders. It is an adventure, and no two people will ever experience life in the same way. No two people will ever react or respond in the same way to similar circumstances. That is the beauty and miracle of life. You are your own creator, and life is like a "choose your own adventure" story. You are the author, and you can dream, believe, and achieve whatever you choose. You are completely responsible for how you choose to live it, no matter what adversities you have faced. Life is a big playground in which there are countless recurring lessons and opportunities presented to us. These are the life patterns that we so often become oblivious to, despite them continuously showing up in our lives in a variety of ways and forms. Repeating themselves until we have an aha moment and learn them, which means we no longer need to repeat the pattern of unhealthy behaviour. It's something that we can finally let go of if we become aware or conscious of this pattern.

Often, we choose not to see them, and we choose not to learn from these repetitive life lessons. Sometimes we choose to stay in the valleys of life and blame others for our situation, but if you want to reach for the stars, you need to stand at the top of the mountain. If you want to get to the top, you need to climb a ladder. To find yourself on top of the mountain, you need to do the work. No one will carry you up there. Like I said, the lessons mean more when you discover them for yourself. There are a few kind-hearted souls who will help you clear the way and lend a helping hand, but the climb is still up to you. What I want you to remember is that, at any given moment, you can choose to change your life story, and you can get yourself out of the valley and start climbing the mountain, or ladder, of life. It's all in the decision. Once the decision is made, you're already halfway there. Keep making choice after choice after choice that are driven by your original decision. Remain focussed.

You will continue to come across a variety of challenges that life will undoubtedly put in your path, but how you deal with them is completely up to you. You might even get to the point where you don't see them, or interpret them, as problems or challenges anymore, realising it's just another chance to learn, and you may even bless them for coming into your life. Thanking the lesson for the blessing. Ultimately testing your unwavering faith!

Instead of asking, "who am I?", you need to ask yourself, "will I let myself stumble? Will I continue to struggle and fall and not get up again, or will I learn from my lessons and use those stumbling blocks as life's stepping stones or ladder?" "Will I continue to grow and climb to new heights, or will I give up all hope, and feel helpless in my circumstances, and stay where I am?"

What I have found on my journey up the mountain of life is that the only person that can help you truly discover "Who am I?" is you, and the only way to finding the joy within is to look deep inside your own soul.

I hope that you have enjoyed following me on my journey to discover "Who am I?" and, in doing so, I hope that I've helped you to "Find the Joy Within."

Glossary and Abbreviations

4WD	Four-wheel drive
Aussie*	Slang and shortened version of Australia
BBQ	Barbeque
CB	Citizen Band (Two-way radio)
Cocky*	A slang word for an Australian farmer
Coconut*	A slang description of an Aboriginal person that is black on the outside, but white on the inside.
DOCS	Department of Families and Communities
IVE	Introductory Vocational Education
Koori	Descriptive word for a person of Aboriginal descent. (New South Wales and Victorian)
NELMIC	New Entry Lecturer's Method Introductory Course
NSW	New South Wales
NT	Northern Territory
Nunga	Descriptive word for a person of Aboriginal descent. (South Australian)
QLD	Queensland
SA	South Australia
SANFL	South Australia National Football League
Shame	To be embarrassed, ashamed, or shy
TAFE	Technical and Further Education
TV	Television

Bibliography

Dyer, W. W. (2010). The Shift: Taking Your Life from Ambition to Meaning. Hay House Australia Pty Ltd.

Hay, L. (1984). You Can Heal Your Life. Hay House, Santa Monica, CA.

The Bible. (Matthew 6:9–13). The Lord's Prayer.

Warren, R. (2002). The Purpose Driven Life: What on Earth Am I Here For? Hyde Park Press, Adelaide, South Australia.

Stone, W. (1998). The Success System That Never Fails. HarperCollins Publishers.